2012 Issue 4

NEW IN CHESS

PUBLISHER: **Allard Hoogland** EDITORS-IN-CHIEF: **Dirk Jan ten Geuzendam, Jan Timman**

10 Anand-Gelfand

32 Interview

85 Malmö

57 U.S. Women's Championship

'Then I went backstage. And suddenly I saw a move, I couldn't see clearly, but it seemed to come from the back of the board. And I looked at the monitor and it said queen f6, and I couldn't believe it, came back. I was trying to calm down, because basically I knew it was over.' – Vishy Anand

CONTRIBUTORS TO THIS ISSUE
Vishy Anand, Fabiano Caruana, Boris Gelfand, Anish Giri, Charles Hertan, Gregory Kaidanov, Taylor Kingston, Vladimir Kramnik, Irina Krush, Peter Leko, Hikaru Nakamura, Peter Heine Nielsen, Yannick Pelletier, Macauley Peterson, Ray Robson, Nigel Short, Jan Timman
PHOTOS AND ILLUSTRATIONS
Boris Dolmatovsky, Calle Erlandsson, chesstv.eu, Anastasia Karlovich, Macauley Peterson, Studio314, Alexey Yushenkov
COVER PHOTO
Vishy Anand: New In Chess

Chess Meets Art

There can be no denying that art was an omnipresent theme at the World Championship match in Moscow. There were lectures, press conferences by art specialists and various exhibitions, and even the live broadcasts were regularly interrupted by videos about highlights from the Tretyakov Gallery. Still, most of those present looked on in wonder when, on one of the last days of the match, Max Dlugy and an assistant walked into the VIP-room and started hanging paintings on the wall. Dlugy's paintings!

Born in Moscow in 1966, Max Dlugy spent his formative years in the U.S., where he built up a promising chess career. He won the World Juniors in 1985, became a grandmaster one year later, claimed tournaments like the World Open, even became President of the U.S. Chess Federation at the age of 23(!), and retired from professional chess in 1990. Having

Markers on cardboard by Dlugy.

worked as a trader at Banker's Trust, he returned to Moscow in the mid-90s to pursue a business career.

Which doesn't mean that he ever forgot about his calling as an artist! Dlugy remembers that he received his first art lessons from his uncle Vitaly when he was about seven years old. 'At that point it was water colours with water to haze the effect and I loved what it did! I always loved to doodle and when my mother, who was always very artistic, became a full-fledged artist at 55, it was very inspiring to try and focus a bit on my own artworks.'

Of late the urge to create has grown notably and his production has increased accordingly. For the moment he doesn't want to limit himself: 'I have tried a number of techniques.

Max Dlugy with 'X marks the spot'.

I would say currently my favourite is markers on cardboard, but I have made paintings with oil, tempera and pencils as well.' As a true artist he describes why he doesn't have any preferred subjects: 'Because the whole idea of what I draw is not to concentrate on something specific but rather to let my own imagination and creativity move me towards an unspecified form or colour.'

So far, Dlugy has not been actively trying to sell his art, but he did give one of his paintings to Anatoly Karpov as a present for his 60th birthday last May. And although he wants to be free in his choice of subjects, it surely comes as no surprise that chess is one of his themes. One of the works he showed during his first public presentation was called 'X marks the spot', inspired by a fantastic queen sacrifice made in 1986 by Alex Shabalov. The x is visible on the b5-square of a chess board and marks the spot where the queen was offered.

As Shabalov's queen sacrifice was a piece of art in its own right, let's have a look at Dlugy's inspiration:

Vetemaa-Shabalov
Haapsalu 1986
position after 20.♗xc4

20...♕b5!! Black threatens 21...♕xb2 mate and offers the queen to be taken in two ways. But in both cases taking the queen is met by 21...♘b3 mate. His opponent tried: **21.♖d2** but after **21...♘xc3** he resigned, as 22.bxc3 runs into 22...♕b1 mate and 22.♕xc3 into 22...♘b3+ 23.♗xb3 ♖xc3+.

Does He Play Chess?

The day after his successful defence of his world title, Vishy Anand and his challenger Boris Gelfand were invited to visit Russian president Vladimir Putin. As Anand related, Putin was well informed and seemed to have followed the match. Or had listened carefully to one of his assistants, of course. Whether the Russian president really plays chess we don't know. About his predecessor, Dmitry Medvedev, we learned from his chief economic ad-

Russian president Vladimir Putin receives Anand and Gelfand.

Chess everywhere for Vladimir Putin and Dmitry Medvedev.

visor Arkady Dvorkovich that he had a chess set in his office and knew the rules, but wasn't really an active player.

Still, all this uncertainty didn't stop an unknown artist producing a se-

COLOPHON

PUBLISHER: Allard Hoogland
EDITORS-IN-CHIEF:
Dirk Jan ten Geuzendam, Jan Timman
EDITORS: Peter Boel, René Olthof
ART-DIRECTION: Jan Scholtus
PRODUCTION: Joop de Groot
TRANSLATORS:
Sarah Hurst, Ken Neat, Piet Verhagen
SALES AND ADVERTISING: Casper Pieters

NEW IN CHESS
P.O. BOX 1093
1810 KB ALKMAAR
THE NETHERLANDS

PHONE: 00-31-(0)72-51 27 137
FAX: 00-31-(0)72-51 58 234
E-MAIL:
SUBSCRIPTIONS: nic@newinchess.com
EDITORS: editors@newinchess.com
SALES AND ADVERTISING:
casper.pieters@newinchess.com

BANK DETAILS:
IBAN: NL41ABNA 0589126024
BIC: ABNANL2A in favour of Interchess BV, Alkmaar, The Netherlands

WWW.NEWINCHESS.COM

ries of paintings in which Putin and Medvedev are seen playing chess. They remind one of the paintings of Lenin and Gorky playing chess and, as was the case with some of those products of 'Soviet realism', we may doubt their historical correctness. Putin and Medvedev enjoy the beauty of our royal game in a variety of settings: at the airport, on top of a snow-covered mountain, on the banks of the Neva, in arctic surroundings with the board atop a sledge, relaxing on a Black Sea beach and sharing a beer in the woods. The paintings were spotted in a clinic in St. Petersburg.

Russian Heritage

One of the exhibitions organized in connection with the world championship match was a small show at the Multimedia Art Museum called 'Chess Pieces of the 20th Century'. On display were rare chess sets, photographs by Boris Dolmatovsky and a fascinating selection of photos from Russian archives. A cou-

Chess at the Pushkin Museum in 1935.

ple of those latter photos were taken at the tournament that inspired Andrey Filatov to have the match in a museum. The International Tournament in Moscow in 1935, won by Botvinnik and Flohr ahead of Lasker and Capablanca, was held in the Pushkin Museum of Fine Arts. According to Filatov, 'because the Soviet government wanted to show the world that it had not sold off its Russian heritage'. ■

'It has been clear for some time now that Russia has lost its pre-eminent position in world chess. Suffice it to look at the results of team tournaments (the Olympiad, world championships) and at those of young chess players. Russia does not have a single "extra-class" player in the over-20 category. When I say "extra class", I mean of world champion calibre.

'The situation in Russia in recent years has not been conducive to development of intellectual disciplines. (..) The current regime in Russia is suspicious of any type of intellectual activity. Russia is facing the biggest wave of emigration since 1917. It does not take great intellectual ability to operate a pipeline.'
Garry Kasparov at a press conference during the World Championship match in Moscow

'(Anand's) match with Topalov was already clearly a drop in quality when you look at the Kramnik match. He survived the match and in some games you saw a sparkle of genius. Very often in the match he was struggling. But now you very often see a "Maginot Line", defensive wall tactics.'
Garry Kasparov during the live broadcast of Game 6 of the match

'Really looking forward to the tiebreak of Anand-Gelfand tomorrow. It's like in football, even after a boring 0-0 draw you want to watch ET.'
Magnus Carlsen on *Twitter*

'Seriously though, I don't blame the players for agreeing to all those early draws, it's just appalling that the rules allow them to.'
Magnus Carlsen on *Twitter* 6 minutes later

Taking Chess to the Museum

If it's up to Russian billionaire Andrey Filatov, having the World Championship match in the Engineering Building of the Tretyakov Gallery (right next to the monumental main entrance) will herald a new trend in chess. Filatov, an ardent collector of paintings himself, is firmly convinced that both chess and art can profit from this liaison and for next year he has announced an Alekhine Memorial that will be split between the Louvre in Paris and a Russian museum. The painting adorning the poster of the match was 'Brigade is taking a rest' by Viktor Popkov (1932-74), which won a Grand Prix during the World Biennale of young artists in Paris in 1961. To Filatov's mind, Popkov is one of many Russian artists who are underrated and therefore under-priced. If their work is popularized, their names will become better known and in the years ahead the prices that they will fetch at auctions will go up significantly.

From his suite on the seventh floor of the Baltschug Kempinski Hotel, World Champion Vishy Anand had a stunning view of the Kremlin and Red Square. This photo was taken on the eve of the festivities on May 9 celebrating the end of World War II.

The 2012 World Championship match set new standards for top-level chess. The felicitous marriage of Andrey Filatov's ambitious vision and the organizational expertise of the Russian Chess Federation produced an unforgettable event at a baffling venue with unprecedented Internet coverage. As he had predicted all along, Vishy Anand had to fight for his life to retain his title at the Tretyakov Gallery and only managed to do so in a scintillating tiebreak. Challenger Boris Gelfand left Moscow with his head up high after 'the best month in his life' and countered criticism of the contestants' play with a heart-felt plea in defence of the grand tradition of chess and its cultural significance.

State of
the Art in
Moscow

W

When I go for breakfast on the day of the tiebreaks, the restaurant of the Baltschug Kempinski is buzzing with activity. All the tables in the main room look occupied. Much to my surprise, one of the waitresses leads me to the side room where Vishy Anand and his team have been having breakfast for the past three weeks. The sign saying 'Anand Team Breakfast' has been removed and as if their special guest left weeks ago she laconically indicates a table in the midst of a lively crowd of business people. Apparently, the prevailing pre-match sentiment that Anand would decide the match in his favour in the 12 classical games has not been totally dispelled everywhere. And as if to further confuse me, two suitcases are sitting next to the entrance to the room.

Anand and his seconds are nowhere to be seen. With good reason. They must be occupied with frantic last-minute preparations for the decisive day of the match. In the preceding weeks breakfast was the only time when the Anand team could be spotted in the Baltschug. And you had to be quick, as they were never around for long, sticking to a Stakhanovite regime that confined them to their rooms for most of the day. Given an option of several hotels, Anand

chose the five-star Baltschug, possibly attracted by the view from the top floor they occupied. Sitting at the chair on which he usually worked, the World Champion only had to raise his eyes to see St. Basil's Cathedral on Red Square.

As with his previous matches, Anand's team consisted of Peter Heine Nielsen, Rustam Kasimdzhanov, Surya Ganguly and Radek Wojtaszek. In one of the live broadcasts, I 'revealed', in my capacity as host of the English commentary, that Pentala Harikrishna was also in Moscow. This 'revelation' certainly shocked Harikrishna, who sat listening in Hyderabad! I must confess that I had fallen victim to a joke of one of the team members that I misunderstood.

Boris Gelfand opted for a less luxurious hotel slightly closer to the venue, the Park Inn, because of the vicinity of a park where he could go for walks. On the free days the challenger also worked on his physical shape playing table tennis. Thanks to the lessons he has been taking three times a week in Israel he had no trouble defeating the seconds he had brought to Moscow: his loyal friends Alexander Khuzman, Pavel Eljanov and Max Rodshtein.

The only person able to keep up with him at table tennis, Gelfand confided, was Michael Roiz, a key member of the team who had stayed at home, but was permanently in touch with his colleagues.

The Baltschug also was the home of the FIDE board members and the Appeals Committee, which was made up of Kurt Jungwirth, Boris Kutin and Jorge Vega. Given the excellent relations between Anand and Gelfand, they didn't expect any work and indeed they had nothing to do. In fact, this title match was a leisure trip for all FIDE officials, as literally everything was taken care of by the professionals of the Russian Chess Federation, the staff of the Tretyakov and other experts, such as the television company that had been hired, and the most capable people around Andrey Filatov. Possibly to stress that everyday work goes on, even during a world championship match, FIDE had asked for an office with a fax machine at the venue, neither of which had been used on the final day of the match.

The grand opening ceremony in the Vrubel Hall of the Tretyakov Gal-

Piano virtuoso Denis Matsuev was the star of the opening ceremony in the Vrubel Hall.

ALEXEY YUSHENKOV

lery set the tone for a match that invoked superlatives from everyone who attended it. The star of the evening was piano virtuoso Denis Matsuev, who treated his audience to dazzling pyrotechnics. Remarkably, Matsuev waived his usual five-figure fee and insisted on performing for free. Among the guests were a handful of Russian billionaires, former President Mikhail Gorbachov, former Finance Minister Alexey Kudrin, President of the Russian Olympic Committee Alexander Zhukov and Arkady Dvorkovich, who had been appointed a deputy prime minster in the new government only days before. And of course there were countless members of the chess community, e.g. Anatoly Karpov, Yuri Averbakh, Klara Kasparova and Alexander Nikitin, to name just a few. One of the billionaires was main sponsor Andrey Filatov, who forked out five million dollars to see his youthful dream ('to take part in the chess world championship') come true, another one his friend Gennady Timchenko, owner of oil trading giant Gunvor, who happily contributed one million. Right away Filatov showed that his wish to connect chess and art was not limited to the choice of the venue, as he presented the Tretyakov Gallery with a unique handcrafted chess set made out of mammoth bone.

The drawing of lots consisted of the players picking a painting brush with which they signed a canvas that depicted a position from a game they had won against each other. Gelfand signed a position from the game he won against Anand in Biel 1993 with black paint, Anand signed a position from the game in which he defeated Gelfand in the same Swiss city four years later with white paint, thus drawing white for the first match game. Following the official part, drinks and snacks were served among the paintings of the Tretyakov, the pride of Moscow museums, a truly unforgettable experience.

ERIC VAN REEM

'Following the official part, drinks and snacks were served among the paintings of the Tretyakov, the pride of Moscow museums, a truly unforgettable experience.'

While the opening ceremony was a privilege for the happy few, the match itself was shared with the entire world in a manner that has not been seen before. The official website brought chess fans everywhere all they could have dreamed of in the best possible quality. Particularly impressive were the live broadcasts in HD that went without a glitch, thanks to the expertise of a highly professional television company specialized in covering big events in Russia. I understand that it sounds a bit suspect to shed such praise on an enterprise that you were involved in yourself, but given the general enthusiasm about this technical achievement I happily take that risk. And of course it was a privilege to talk about the games and listen to the assessments of the dream team of grandmaster commentators that were invited.

For the English broadcasts, which on average were watched by some 225,000 viewers, the regular GM commentators were Nigel Short, Jan Timman, Joel Lautier, Peter Svidler, Peter Leko and Vladimir Kramnik. The sur-

ANASTASIA KARLOVICH

Watched by his daughter, Andrey Filatov talks to a Russian television channel.

Boris Gelfand and Vishy Anand found it difficult to enjoy the press conferences. Moments of silence and annoyed glances frequently created an uncomfortable atmosphere.

ALEXEY YUSHENKOV

prise guests included Garry Kasparov, Anatoly Karpov, Sergey Karjakin, Ian Nepomniachtchi and Alexander Morozevich. What more could you hope for?

An essential feature of the commentary was that the grandmasters gave their views without any kind of computer assistance. The emphasis was on explaining what was happening in the games to a broad audience, not on commenting on the assessments of Houdini or any other engine. Still, for those who preferred lifeless computer assessments, the website also offered a game viewer together with Houdini analysis.

The advantage of following a game together with a world class grandmaster without a computer is that you get much closer to the tension that builds in a game. The obvious risk is that at times you miss a hidden tactic that is immediately visible to spectators at home with an engine running. This is what happened in Game 8, when it took Peter Leko and Ian Nepomniachtchi, two 2700+ players, some time to lose their initial enthusiasm about Gelfand's 14...♕f6 and realize that, in fact, it was a losing move because of 17.♕f2. The good thing was that it made Gelfand's oversight understandable and human. Instead of joining the choir of computer-armed amateurs who cried out how

a player of Gelfand's level could make such a mistake, Leko said that he hoped Boris would watch the video of the commentary and find some solace in the fact that he wasn't the only strong player who assessed 14...♕f6 wrongly.

Something similar happened in the third rapid game, when Gelfand could have won a piece with 25.♘xe4,

> 'An essential feature of the commentary was that the grandmasters gave their views without any kind of computer assistance'

a move both he, Anand and the online commentators, all left to their own devices, had missed. Sadly, this high-level shared chess blindness didn't stop a chess columnist, and no doubt he was not the only one, from haughtily calling 25.♘xe4 'not that difficult to see'.

Following the games move by move while listening to the thoughts of great experienced players had the added advantage of making you feel part of the struggle and giving you a better feeling for the decisions the World Champion and his challenger were taking, without falling for the cynicism that prevailed after a number of games had ended in relatively short draws. Likewise, it was easier to understand what Levon Aronian meant when he explained that you had to see the entire match as one big game.

One of the most outspoken critics, particularly of the play Vishy Anand was showing, was Garry Kasparov, who joined the commentary during Game 6. According to the 13th World Champion, his Indian successor lacked motivation, a statement he had also made at the press conference earlier in the afternoon. Referring to a comment by an Indian journalist who was not pleased by his criticism, Kasparov said: 'I think the Indian chess players should be disappointed, not with my statements but with the kind of chess Anand is playing. As for the pressure on Mr. Anand today, I would like to remind you that Karpov and I had played more matches in a shorter period of time, which did not prevent us from remaining numbers one and two in world chess.'

Kasparov was one of Anand's three secret helpers during his match against Topalov in Sofia two years ago. This time Magnus Carlsen had good personal grounds to stay neutral, as had Vladimir Kramnik, who is a good friend of both Anand and Gelfand. In Kasparov's case there was no doubt he would not support Anand this time either. Although this was never explicitly pronounced, he had expected that his support during the match against Topalov would persuade Anand to openly support him and Karpov in the FIDE presidential elections in Khanty-Mansiysk. When Anand did not return this favour, Kasparov did not hide his disappoint-

Minsk 1989. Together with two friends, Andrey Filatov (left) and Ilya Smirin (2nd from right), students at the Institute for Physical Culture, hold a boa constrictor.

ment. This time he remained a neutral observer, although, quite remarkably, Boris Gelfand revealed in an interview with ChessVibes that he had been approached by people around Kasparov with a proposal for close collaboration before and during the match.

The host of the Russian commentary was Israeli GM Ilya Smirin, like Gelfand an old friend of Filatov's. His guests, apart from the same Peter Svidler and Vladimir Kramnik, included Sergey Rublevsky, Alexander Grischuk and Dmitry Jakovenko. At breakfast in the Baltschug, Ilya spoke with enthusiasm about the plans of Filatov to reshape the economy of chess by teaming up with museums and shared memories of his days at the Institute for Physical Culture in Minsk, where he and Gelfand and Filatov were students. One anecdote that Filatov likes to remind him of was connected to the popular Soviet film The Irony of Fate, which plays on the uniformity of Soviet architecture and tells about a drunk Muscovite who is put on a plane and ends up in a similar flat as his own in Leningrad. In 1990, when Smirin went to pick up his bride for his first marriage, he also got confused by similarly looking buildings and rang a doorbell in the wrong apartment block. Filatov still hap-

pily remembers how the woman who opened the door, upon seeing a young man in his best suit who asked for Olga, enthusiastically turned around and shouted, come daughter, there is someone for you!

The criticism about the level of the match that briefly disappeared when Gelfand took the lead in Game 7

> ## Gelfand stopped Anand from playing his best. Or, as the challenger put it himself: 'Every player plays as strongly as his opponent allows him'

and Anand hit back with a historically short 17-move win the next day, returned when despite interesting opening strategies the remaining four classical games ended in draws again and tiebreaks became necessary. There was little appreciation for

the fact that with his active black play and his cleverly thought out choice of the Grünfeld and the Sveshnikov as his main weapons Gelfand stopped Anand from playing his best. Or, as the challenger put it himself: 'Every player plays as strongly as his opponent allows him and by playing these aggressive openings I didn't allow him to show his best and get positions in which he is so good.'

Regular visitor Mark Dvoretsky even questioned the match format. 'The match as the ideal test of strength was Botvinnik's conviction, who would say it was the best for chess. But whenever Botvinnik said something was the best for chess, he actually meant that it was the best for Botvinnik. These days, with two teams preparing so deeply, it is no longer a conflict between two players. On top of that the advantage of the champion is unreasonable.'

Part of the criticism may have been invoked by Anand's presentation at the board and during the press conferences. Although the rules required that the players wear suits during the games, the World Champion appeared in the same shirt or sweater of his sponsor that he has been wearing for the last few years, creating the impression that his sponsor had not bothered to provide him with anything new for this special occasion. At the press conferences he often showed discomfort and frequently declined to answer questions. Many of these questions were fairly silly or difficult to answer seriously, but still these silences and annoyed glances created an uncomfortable atmosphere.

The tension and excitement of the tiebreaks couldn't fully take away the disappointment of the majority of the press corps, but certainly provided good compensation. All four games were nail-biters and it was a small miracle that only Game 2 ended in a decision, a decision in favour of Vishy Anand, who kept his title in the closest match he has played so far.

As Anand and his team celebrated, more and more observers expressed their admiration for the fight his challenger put up. Finally the realization fully sank in that Anand's repeatedly expressed respect for his opponent had not been a stock reaction, empty words of praise to protect himself from overconfidence, but a sincere appreciation of his talent and strength.

Gelfand himself remained admirably true to himself and not disappointed in the least when I asked him for an evaluation. 'I came to play a big match and I was playing it with dignity and motivation, from the first game to the last game of the tiebreak. I played a great match and I am proud of my achievement. I was written off 15 years ago and people keep on doing it. When I qualified from Kazan they were saying the system was wrong. Like Winnie the Pooh was saying, wrong bees are making the wrong honey. I played well, but you saw Barcelona-Chelsea, Messi hits the post from a penalty, what can you do? It's sport. You have to accept it and continue. The title is not the main thing in life. The effort is much more important for me.'

'It was written on one website that the match was not as entertaining as the Eurovision Song Contest. That was a good point. We should not compete with Eurovision, we should compete with classical music, we should keep high standards. This is what was missing. There were around 400 journalists and only 10 to 15 showed professionalism. This is the key problem. For the moment we have millions of spectators all over the world, who enjoy the game and follow it. I think it's important to keep these millions rather than make our chess primitive and get 10 million more, people who watch it eating pizza and drinking cola if we manage to compete with Eurovision.'

'Every day my team made a press survey for me, with good humour. What nonsense was written, who praised the game. Yesterday I saw a

A gift for the World Champion, the painting that Andrey Filatov commissioned from Russian modern impressionist Yuri Krotov.

discussion between Mig Greengard and Levon Aronian. When Levon praised us, Mig Greengard ridiculed him and said that it was a boring match. And Levon correctly pointed out that the less a person knows about

> 'Of course, people who don't make an intellectual effort don't believe in me.'

a subject the more he treats it with disrespect. For me the opinion of Levon Aronian or other people that love chess is more important than a thousand Mig Greengards together.'

'Titles have never been important to me. Not even now I was so close. To play such a great match was one of my dreams coming true. And especially to play it in such a brilliant museum with so much attention from real chess lovers around the world. It was really the best month in my life. The only thing I regret is that now I have to work very

hard to earn another match. I know this is contrary to what most of the world thinks possible, but a lot of people believe in me. Of course, people who don't make an intellectual effort don't believe in me. People who want to think by other people's standards, in clichés, they don't believe it. And I always fight against all the clichés.'

The closing ceremony was a worthy farewell of a historic event, with moving footage of the highlights, spectacular trophies and two more gifts from Andrey Filatov: one painting showing Denis Matsuev in action at the opening ceremony for the Tretyakov Gallery and one painting showing Anand and Gelfand at the board for the old and new world champion. They were commissioned from Russian modern impressionist Yuri Krotov, who had had three weeks to paint them.

When I go for breakfast the next morning, the sign saying 'Anand Team Breakfast' is back in place. The entire team is in the room and Vishy Anand is the radiant centre of attention. Relaxed and upbeat he is cracking jokes and chess variations are exchanged at lightning speed. Peter Heine Nielsen and Hans Walter Schmitt are wearing Vishy Anand World Champion T-shirts. Subtitle: simply the best. As if they never doubted this.

NOTES BY
Boris Gelfand

SL 8.1 – D45
Boris Gelfand
Vishy Anand
Moscow 2012 (7)

1.d4 d5 2.c4 c6 3.♘c3 ♘f6 4.e3 e6 5.♘f3 a6 6.c5

In the three preceding games of the match I was unable to achieve any real advantage after either 6.b3 or 6.♕c2. For this game together with my seconds I had prepared a new continuation.
6...♘bd7

7.♕c2!? The idea of this useful move is prophylactic.

The experience of recent years has shown that after 7.b4 Black equalizes by ...b6, while if 7.♗d3, then ...e5 is strong, with good play for Black.

After the text-move White is ready to respond in various ways to each of Black's possible plans.

7...b6

The play takes on a different character after 7...e5 8.dxe5 ♘g4 9.e6 fxe6 10.♗d3 ♘gf6 (10...♘de5!?) 11.♘g5 ♘xc5 12.♗xh7 ♘xh7 13.♕g6+ ♔d7 14.♘f7, with advantage to White, Radjabov-Grischuk, Bastia 2003.

8.cxb6 ♘xb6 9.♗d2 c5 10.♖c1

In view of the threat of 11.dxc5 ♗xc5 12.♘xd5 White forces Black to determine the pawn structure.

The immediate opening of the c-file doesn't bring anything real: 10.dxc5 ♗xc5 11.♖c1 ♗e7. Black's pawn majority in the centre gives him good counter-chances.

10...cxd4

In the event of 10...c4 11.b3, thanks to his lead in development, White is better prepared for play on the queenside. (Apparently Anand did not agree with the need for passive defence and he prepared another type of pawn structure, which outwardly is completely safe for Black.) To avoid creating a weakness for himself on c4, Black has to agree to the exchange 11...cxb3 12. axb3 ♗b7 13.♗d3 ♗d6 14.0-0 0-0 15. ♘e5 ♖c8 16.♕b2 and White retains a slight positional advantage thanks to the better placing of his pieces.

11.exd4 ♗d6

In this position White has a choice between playing for a positional advantage and an interesting attempt to exploit the tactical features of the position.

12.♗g5

12.♘a4!? forces events, since Black's reply is practically obligatory: 12... ♘xa4 13.♕c6+ ♗d7 14.♕xd6.

ANALYSIS DIAGRAM

At this critical moment Black has a choice between 14...♘xb2 and 14... ♘e4.

14...♘xb2 looks dangerous. After 15.♕a3 ♘c4 16.♗xc4 dxc4 17.♗a5 White detains the black king in the centre, which gives him a dangerous initiative.

The continuation 14...♘e4 leads to simplification and a small advantage

for White in the endgame, but Black retains a defensible position: 15.♕a3 ♘xd2 16.♔xd2!? ♕e7 17.♕xe7+ ♔xe7 18.b3 ♘b6 19.♖c5 f6.

12...0-0 13.♗d3 h6 14.♗h4 ♗b7 15.0-0

15...♕b8?!

A rather risky strategic decision by Anand. After 15...♗f4, depriving White of the important c1-square, Black would practically have equalized:

ANALYSIS DIAGRAM

For instance 16.♖b1 ♘bd7 17.b4 ♖c8 18.♕b3 ♘b6 or 16.♖cd1 ♘bd7 17. ♘a4 a5 18.♘c5 ♕b6.

Black sets White a difficult strategic choice: either to play for an attack by 16.♗xf6 at the cost of giving Black the advantage of the bishop pair and pawn control of the centre, or to follow the general strategic course of play against the 'bad' ♗b7, for which 16.♗g3 should be chosen. I took the decision in favour of the second continuation, in full accordance with my understanding of chess, which to a great extent was formed under the influence of the games of Akiba Rubinstein, my favourite chess player from the past.

A determined and focused Boris Gelfand arrives at the back entrance of the Engineering Building of the Tretyakov Gallery.

ERIC VAN REEM

16.♗g3!? After 16.♗xf6!? gxf6 17. ♘e2! is the best way of continuing the attack. Black faces a difficult defence: 17...♖c8 18.♕d2 ♗f8 19.♖xc8 ♘xc8 (or 19...♕xc8 20.♘f4, with initiative) 20.♘g3 ♘d6 21.♘h5 ♗g7 22.♕f4 ♘e4 23.♕g4 ♘g5 24.♘xg5 fxg5 25. ♘xg7 ♔xg7 26.f4, and despite the numerous exchanges, White retains a dangerous initiative.

16...♖c8 17.♕e2 ♗xg3 18.hxg3

At this point the computer does not give White any advantage, and therefore many confused commentators did not assess the position properly. Despite the apparent simplicity of the position, Black has to defend accurately against a whole series of strategic ideas for White: the doubling

of rooks on the c-file, the invasion of the ♘f3 on e5, a pawn attack on the queenside by a3-b4, and possible activity on the kingside with the inclusion of f4 and g4-g5. A considerable role in Black's problems is played by the ♗b7, which in fact remained out of play and as a result led to his defeat. In the given position the attempt to play for an attack by 18.fxg3 is unconvincing, and it leads merely to a weakening of White's pawn structure, without giving any real attacking chances in return.

18...♕d6

18...♖c7 19.♖c2 ♕a7 would not have solved Black's problems. I considered two possibilities for White:

ANALYIS DIAGRAM

A) 20.♕e5 ♗c6 21.♕f4 ♖ac8 22. ♖fc1 is an interesting set-up, by which White maintains the status quo on the queenside and can develop his initiative on the kingside, exploiting the better placing of his pieces and the good communications between them;

B) The straightforward plan of playing on the queenside is even stronger: 20.♖fc1 ♖ac8 21.b3 ♘bd7 22.♘a4.

ANALYSIS DIAGRAM

To bring his ♗b7 into play, Black is forced to play ...a5. Then after ♗b5 at any moment White can transpose into a favourable piece arrangement with knight against bishop: 22...♖xc2 23.♖xc2 a5 24.♗b5 ♕b8 25.♗xd7 ♘xd7 26.♘c5 ♘xc5 27.♖xc5 ♖xc5 28.dxc5 ♗c8 29.♕e3, and in my opinion the ♕+♘ are stronger than the ♕+♗ in this position. Even if Black should succeed in playing f6-e5, with f4 White will be able to securely block Black's central pawns, and White's pawns on the queenside will decide the game in his favour.

19.♖c2

19.♘e5 suggests itself, but the move turns out to be pseudo-active: 19... ♖c7 20.♖c2 ♘fd7 21.♖fc1 ♘xe5 22. dxe5 ♕d8 gives Black good play.

19...♘bd7

The set-up 19...♘fd7 20.♖fc1 ♗c6 would have insured Black against

immediate problems, but also White would have retained opportunities for play both on the queenside with b3-a4, and also on the kingside with the possible pawn advance g4-g5. Also, the simple exchange of rooks by 21.♘d1 would have left White with an advantage in the endgame.

19...a5 is premature, since the removal of control from the b5-point assists White's play: 20.♖fc1 ♕e7 21.a3, intending 21...♘c4 22.♘a4!, with initiative. White's play on the queenside is only helped by 19...♘c4 20.♘a4 ♘d7 21.♖fc1.

20.♖fc1

20...♖ab8?!

An aimless move, which allows White to seize the initiative on the queenside. The attempt to gain counterplay by 20...♖e8 allows White to fight for an advantage in two ways – by allowing or preventing 21...e5:

Long **Awaited**
2nd edition
ECE I
PAWN ENDINGS
Chess Informant SINCE 1966

Hardback | 455 pages | € 32.00 | Available at your local bookseller or at www.chessinformant.rs

ANALYSIS DIAGRAM

A) 21.♘e5!? ♛b4 22.♕e3 (intending a3-b4 and ♘a4) 22...♘xe5 23.dxe5 ♘d7 24.♗e2 and White has a classic advantage;

B) 21.♘a4 e5, and now White retains a small advantage after 22.dxe5 ♘xe5 23.♘c5.

In my opinion the best set-up for Black is 20...♖c7!, intending ...♖ac8. Now, in order to obtain even a minimal advantage, great accuracy is demanded of White:

ANALYSIS DIAGRAM

A) Black exploits the fact that 21.♘b5 does not work: 21...♖xc2 22.♘xd6 ♖xc1+ 23.♗e1 ♖b8, and only Black may be better;

B) White does not gain any advantage by 21.a3 ♖ac8 22.b4 a5! (this accurate move, demanding good calculation, enables Black to obtain an equal game) 23.bxa5 ♕xa3 24.a6 ♖xc3 25.♖xc3 ♖xc3 26.♖xc3 ♕xc3 27.axb7 ♕b8. Black neutralizes the b7-pawn without difficulty after 28.♕e5 ♘fd7 29.♕e2 ♘f6;

C) The immediate 21.♘a4 allows Black to exchange his most problematic piece – the bishop on b7: 21...

♖xc2 22.♖xc2 ♗c6! 23.♘c5 ♗b5 24. a3 ♗xd3 25.♕xd3 a5 26.♕b3 ♕b8 27.♕xb8+ ♖xb8, and Black maintains equality in the endgame without any great difficulty;

D) I would have had to find the only move 21.♕e1!?, retaining the initiative after 21...♖ac8 22.♘a4 ♖xc2 23.♗xc2 (intending b4 and ♘c5) 23... ♗c6 24.♘c5 ♕b8 25.b4.

21.♘a4
White could have permitted himself to strengthen his position a little more by 21.♕e3!? ♘b6 22.b3, when Black has absolutely no counterplay.

21...♘e4?!
21...♖xc2 was better, when both 22.♕xc2 and 22.♖xc2 retain an advantage for White, but it would be easier for Black to defend.

22.♖xc8+ ♗xc8
A pawn would have been lost after 22...♖xc8 23.♖xc8+ ♗xc8 24.♗xe4 dxe4 25.♕xe4.

23.♕c2!
A logical and strong move – White purposefully pursues the course of exploiting Black's bad piece, the c8-bishop, which will be especially noticeable in the endgame.

23.♕e1!, suggested by Anatoly Karpov, also looks strong. The white queen goes to a5 with great effect, after which Black's defence becomes very difficult: 23...♗b7 24.♕a5.

23...g5?
This looks strange, but it is hard to suggest a sensible continuation for Black. White has a clear advantage after 23...♗b7 24.♘c5 ♖c8 25.b4. The most resilient looks to be 23... ♘df6. Now White has several promising ways of developing his initiative:

ANALYSIS DIAGRAM

A) After 24.a3 ♗d7 25.♘c5 a5 26. ♘e5 ♗e8 Black regroups his pieces quite well, and it is not easy for White to increase his advantage, for example: 27.♗xe4 dxe4 28.♖d1 ♕d5 29.b3 ♗b5 30.a4 ♗c6 (Black retains chances of counterplay) 31.♘xe6 ♕xe6 32. ♘xc6 ♕xb3 33.♕xb3 ♖xb3 34.♖a1 ♖d3 35.♘xa5 ♖xd4 36.♘b3 ♖d3 37. ♖b1 with a slight advantage;

B) It is promising first to play 24.♘e5 with the idea of later invading on the c-file in combination with ♘c5. However, in this case after 24... ♗d7 25.♘c5 Black retains defensive resources:

ANALYSIS DIAGRAM

25...♘xc5 (also interesting is 25... ♗e8!? when it is risky to play 26. ♘xa6 ♖a8 27.♘c7 ♖c8!, as it is hard for White to disentangle himself) 26.♕xc5 ♕xc5 27.dxc5 ♗b5 28. ♗xb5 axb5 – White has an advantage, but there is no complete certainty that it is sufficient for a win. Black plays his ♘f6 to c7 and can defend with chances of success;

C) 24.♘c5 ♘xc5 suggests itself, when concrete factors allow White to play for the maximum: 25.dxc5! ♕c7 26.♕c3 ♘g4! (Black must prepare active counterplay in the centre) 27.♖e1 a5 and now 28.c6!? leads to a clear advantage for White without any complications.

24.♕c7

White consistently carries out his plan. 24.♘c5 f5 25.b4 would also have led to an advantage.

24...♕xc7?!

24...♗b7 is bad in view of 25.♗xe4 ♕xc7 26.♗h7+! (an important interposition) 26...♔xh7 27.♖xc7 ♔g7 28. ♖xd7 ♗c6 29.♖xf7+! ♔xf7 30.♘e5+ ♔e8 31.♘xc6 ♖c8 32.♘e5 ♖c1+ 33.♔h2 ♖d1 34.♘c5 ♖xd4 35.♘ed3, with a clear advantage for White.

25.♖xc7

White has a strategically winning position. It is hard for Black to avoid

the exchange of his pair of knights for White's bishop and knight, after which the strategic idea of White's play is fully revealed – the advantage of the white knight over the c8-bishop.

25...f6?

This quickly leads to a hopeless position for Black, but in a bad position there are no good moves! (Anand). After 25...♘ef6 26.♘c5 ♖a8 27.b4 Black is helpless.

He also has a difficult position after 25...g4 26.♘e5 ♘xe5 27.dxe5 intending 28.♗e4.

In the event of 25...♘d6 26.♘c5 ♘f6 27.b3 Black is paralysed and loss of material is inevitable.

26.♗xe4!

This timely exchange leads to a position where the white knights are completely dominant.

26...dxe4 27.♘d2 f5 28.♘c4 ♘f6
28...♔f8 29.♘c5 ♘xc5 30.dxc5 e5 31.

c6 ♗e6 32.♖b7 ♖c8 33.♘xe5 was also bad.

29.♘c5 ♘d5 30.♖a7 ♘b4

Or 30...♘f6 31.b3, winning.

31.♘e5?!

Not the most accurate move, but good enough to win.

31.♘d6 ♘d5 (31...♘xa2 32.♖c7) 32.b3 wins. White's winning plan is to advance a4-a5, play his king to the centre to neutralize the black pawns, and after the exchange on c8 to play ♖a6, when the white queenside pawns decide the outcome.

31...♘c2!

Anand exploits the micro-chance offered.

32.♘c6 ♖xb2 33.♖c7

33...♖b1+?

Black would have gained saving chances after 33...e3 34.fxe3 ♘xe3 35.♖xc8+ ♔h7 36.♖c7+ ♔h8 37.♘e5 ♖xg2+ 38.♔h1 ♖f2 when White would be winning after 39.♘cd3, but after 39.♘f7+ ♔g7 40.♘xg5+ ♔g6 41.♘h3 ♖f1+ 42.♘g1 f4 43.gxf4 ♖xf4 the material is reduced, even if White retains chances of success with 44.♖g7+ ♔f6 45.♖g3.

34.♔h2 e3 35.♖xc8+ ♔h7 36.

♖c7+ With his small army White mounts a mating attack.

36...♔h8

37.♘e5

Also possible was 37.♘d7 ♔g7 38.♘ce5 (intending 39.♘f6+ ♔xf6 40.♖f7 mate) 38...♘xd4 39.♘f6+! (this spectacular move, forcing mate in a few moves, would have pleased the spectators, but I would most probably have played 39.fxe3, winning) 39...♔xf6 40.f4 ♘f3+ 41.gxf3 ♖b2+ 42.♔h3 g4+ 43.fxg4 fxg4 44.♔xg4 h5+ 45.♔f3 ♖f2+ 46.♔e4 and mate is inevitable.

37...e2

Or 37...exf2 38.♘xe6 ♖h1+ (38...f1♘+ 39.♔h3 g4+ 40.♔h4) 39.♔xh1 f1♕+ 40.♔h2, winning.

38.♘xe6!

Black resigned in view of 38...e1♕ 39.♘g6+ ♔g8 40.♖g7 mate, or 38...♖h1+ 39.♔xh1 e1♕+ 40.♔h2, winning.

I am pleased that in a match for the World Championship I was able to conduct a game in the style of Akiba Rubinstein, where the entire strategic course was maintained from the first to the last move.

NOTES BY
Vishy Anand

KI 81.3 – E60
Vishy Anand
Boris Gelfand
Moscow 2012 2012 (8)

1.d4 ♘f6 2.c4 g6 3.f3 c5!?

The point of this move is that it forces a Benoni, as 3...♗g7 4.e4 c5, for instance, allows 5.♘e2 options.

4.d5 d6 5.e4 ♗g7 6.♘e2!? 0-0 7.♘ec3

This is a normal concept in Benoni structures, but of course now, without the c4-square available, it is even more double-edged.

7...♘h5 8.♗g5

The tempting alternative was 8.g4!?. This move could be good or bad, but I thought it would not surprise Gelfand. So I thought about something that he might not have looked at in great detail and stumbled on the text-move.

8...♗f6!?

This surprised me. At least some people thought it was clever, but I was actually happy to have the dark-

squared bishop off my back, which I didn't think would be unfavourable for me.

Another idea was 8...h6!? 9.♗h4!? (or 9.♗e3, when after 9...f5 – 9...e6 10.♕d2 looks decent – 10.exf5!? gxf5 11.♕d2 it's not clear where Black's aggression leads) 9...♘d7, which looks OK for Black to me.

9.♗xf6

Even 9.♗e3, followed by ♕d2, a4 and ♘a3, etc., looked reasonable to me during the game, but because of the tactics after 11.exf5! and 12.g4!, I think taking on f6 is better.

9...exf6

This came as a slight surprise, but it's a common motif in the Maroczy Accelerated Dragon.

10.♕d2

This was a very important decision. The main alternative is 10.g4 ♘f4 11.♕d2 g5 12.h4 ♘d7, and I couldn't see any point to White's play. If I take on g5 and go ♕h2, Black simply goes ...h5, puts the second knight on e5, and with one knight on e5, one knight on f4 and a queen potentially on f6 it looks horrible for White. After 12.h4 I can maybe play 13.h5 and pretend that that knight on f4 has nowhere to go, but it didn't convince me at all.

I thought for a while about 10.g4 and was surprised to realize that a lot of people thought this was better than 10.♕d2.

10...f5 11.exf5! ♗xf5

Black cannot play 11...♕h4+ 12.♔d1 ♘g3? because of 13.♕f2 ♘xf5 14.♕xh4 ♘xh4 15.♘b5!, and he loses material.

12.g4

A wealth of World Championship match experience: Vishy Anand and his wife Aruna.

ANASTASIA KARLOVICH

12...♖e8+?!

As usual, a small mistake is soon followed by a bigger one.

He should have tried 12...♗xb1 13.♖xb1 ♘g7!? (13...♘f6 14.h4 is just pleasant. The king goes to c2 or f2 and White will attack) 14.h4 h5 15.♔d1, and despite the fact that Black gets a knight on e5, White has an attack after 15...♘d7 16.♔c2 ♘e5 17.♗e2.

13.♔d1

One of the reasons to go for 10.♕d2 was the line with 13.♔d1. I don't remember if at the point of playing 10.♕d2 I already saw 17.♕f2 or only 17.♕f4, but one way or another I decided that this was something that was quite reasonable for White. My basic thought was that if my king goes to d1 and c2, it should be completely safe and it should be just a little bit unpleasant for Black. I didn't know how huge it was, but certainly thought White was better. I had certainly seen 17.♕f2 by the time I played 12.g4. If I had not seen this move, I might have considered 13.♗e2.

ANALYSIS DIAGRAM

(Editorial note: A beautiful line that Gelfand had been looking at after 13.

♗e2 was 13...♕h4+ 14.♔d1 ♗xb1 15.♖xb1 ♘f6 16.♘b5 ♘a6 17.♘xd6 ♖e7 18.a3 ♖d8 19.♘b5 h5

ANALYSIS DIAGRAM

20.g5 ♘e4! 21.fxe4 ♕xe4, and both rooks are hanging.)

13...♗xb1 14.♖xb1

Knowing that Black's next move was a losing one, I could barely believe it when I saw it appear on the monitor backstage.

14...♕f6??

The lesser evil was 14...♘f6, when after 15.h4 the king on d1 helps White, while the rook on e8 is hardly better placed.

15.gxh5

The obvious move, as I had seen 17.♕f2. In my earlier calculations I didn't spend more than a second on 15.♔c2 ♘f4 16.♘e4, as now the exchange sac 16...♖xe4 leaves Black with a very comfortable position.

15...♕xf3+ 16.♔c2 ♕xh1

'Knowing that Black's next move was a losing one, I could barely believe it when I saw it appear on the monitor backstage.'

17.♕f2!

Initially I had also seen 17.♕f4, to which Black might reply 17...♕g1, but then I j'adoubed the queen to f2 and the alternative became redundant. Obviously Boris had missed 17.♕f2 and he resigned.

NOTES BY
Peter Heine Nielsen

SI 31.4 – B30
Vishy Anand
Boris Gelfand
Moscow 2012 (tiebreak-2)

Before we go ahead and have a look at the second game of the tiebreak that decided the World Championship match, I'd like to take the opportunity to look back at the obstacles Gelfand had to overcome to get this far. His route to Moscow consisted of no fewer than 10 KO-victories, statistically a well-nigh impossible feat, probably only equalled by Vishy's streak in the Groningen and New Delhi FIDE knock-outs. While Fischer's route to the World Championship match consisted of 55(!) and Kasparov's of 51 games, routes shortened by both of them winning their matches in fewer than the required number of games, we now seem to think that quite a number of players should be seeded to a stage where 14 games is enough. Gelfand, however, had to play 56 games to qualify, the longest route ever for a World Championship challenger, and a truly majestic feat to accomplish.

1.e4 c5 2.♘f3 ♘c6 3.♗b5 e6 4. ♗xc6!? Interestingly enough, Gelfand got the bishop pair in no fewer than 9(!) of the games after the opening phase. In modern chess the bishop pair is almost considered a material advantage, but here, as in at least the majority of the other games, Vishy has structural compensation.

4...bxc6

5.b3!? Continuing the discussion from Game 10. In Game 12 we saw 5. d3 ♘e7 6.b3!? d6 7.e5 ♘g6 8.h4! ♘xe5 9.♘xe5 dxe5 10.♘d2

ANALYSIS DIAGRAM

10...c4!!, a move sequence hardly mentioned by any commentator, but in my opinion it contains both some very deep preparation from Vishy's side (including a purely positional pawn-sac) and a very strong over-the-board response from Gelfand, played after a 40-minute think, that kept him in the game, and therefore the match.

5...e5
As in Game 10. Here 5...♘e7 is met by 6.♗a3 ♘g6 7.d4, leading to structures generally pleasant for White.
Gelfand's move is indeed very rare, and forces a reaction from White, as he cannot allow Black to reinforce his centre with 6...d6. This is why 5...d6 would have to be met by 6.e5!.

6.♘xe5 ♕e7

7.d4!?
Game 10 saw 7.♘c4 d5! 8.♘e3 d4 9. ♘c4 ♕xe4+ 10.♕e2 ♕xe2+, with an endgame in which White's structure seemed to give him a pleasant edge. But the bishop pair did indeed turn

The A-Team celebrates once again: Peter Heine Nielsen, Radek Wojtaszek, Aruna Anand, Surya Ganguly, Eric van Reem, Hans-Walter Schmitt and Rustam Kasimdzhanov.

out to outweigh this, and Gelfand's readiness to repeat this game shows his belief in the black position.

7...d6 7...f6!? is a more critical response. White is basically forced into 8.♘f3 ♕xe4+ 9.♔d2!? if he wants to fight for an advantage. The white king will find safety at b2, or at times even at g1 eventually, but White is mainly ready to attack with ♖e1, ♘c3 and ♗a3, which would lead to a very sharp, interesting and irrational battle. Gelfand, however, keeps it sane.

8.♘xc6 ♕xe4+ 9.♕e2 ♕xe2+ 10.♔xe2 ♗b7
The natural reaction. The computers suggest 10...♘e7?!, but after 11.♘xe7 ♗xe7 12.♗e3 it is hard to imagine Black's compensation is even close to sufficient.

11.♘a5!
Immediately returning the pawn and fighting for the initiative.
11.d5?! ♘e7 12.♘xe7 ♗xe7 gives Black excellent compensation, as White can only defend d5 clumsily, since the natural 13.c4? loses to 13...♗f6.

11...♗xg2 12.♖g1

12...♗h3

After a couple of minutes' thought, Gelfand comes up with the best practical choice.

12...♗e4 13.dxc5 dxc5 14.♘c3! would increase White's advantage in development at the price of an unimportant pawn, with a serious white initiative.

13.dxc5 dxc5 14.♘c3 0-0-0

Five minutes of thought, but the right reaction.

15.♗f4

15...♗d6!?

And six more, leaving Gelfand with 11 minutes, while Vishy had almost 25. However, the time was well spent, and as in Game 12, Gelfand takes strong counter-measures and sacrifices a pawn just before Vishy's initiative grows to unstoppable proportions. Allowing moves like ♖ad1 or ♘b5 would soon have left Black's king in a mating net. Now he gets counterplay against White's monarch instead.

16.♗xd6 ♖xd6

17.♖g5 White has quite some options here, and Vishy goes for the attack on the c5-pawn.

Another approach was to fight for the initiative with 17.♘c4!? ♖e6+ 18.♔d2 ♗f5 19.♖ad1. This approach also has

its points, as White's king will be safe on c1, while Black's will still be under attack.

17...♘f6! 18.♖xc5+ ♔b8

White is a clear pawn up, but Black has a certain amount of counterplay, and where before it was definitely Black who had to be careful about his king, this burden now rests on Vishy.

19.♘c4 19.♘b5 is the computer's preferred move, but after 19...♖d7 Black keeps decent chances.

19...♖e8+

20.♘e3 20.♔f3 is another computer idea, but again Black easily keeps his counterplay, with 20...♖d4 21.♖g1 ♗g4+! 22.♔g2 ♗c8 being a possible variation.

On the whole, White will probably be able to create a moderate edge with exact play, but from a practical perspective it's easier being Black.

20...♘g4 21.♘d5 ♘xe3

Black could take on h2, but 22.♖h1 secures a solid plus. Now, however, White is faced with a difficult choice.

22.♘xe3?! 22.fxe3!? looks odd, but it does create some kind of shelter for the king and was generally recommended as a better option. Black

seems reasonably OK, but White is still absolutely safe, with chances for more, whereas now, in the game, all three results have become possible.

22...♗g4+!

Loosening White's foothold.

23.f3 ♗c8 24.♖e1

This move took Vishy four minutes, but despite looking artificial, it is the strongest move, taking prophylactic measures against the pin on the e-file.

24...♖h6

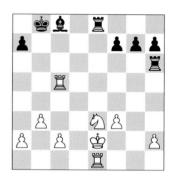

25.♖h1!

Now this is possible, as 25...♗a6+ can be met by 26.♔d2, the point of luring the black rook to h6.

25...♖he6

25...♗b7!?, with the idea of ...♗xf3+, followed by ♖h3+, winning back the piece, leads to instant equality.

26.♖c3 f5 27.♔d2 f4 28.♘d5 g5 29.♖d3 ♖e2+ 30.♔c1 ♖f2 31.h4!

Gelfand used more than half his remaining three and a half minutes here. And although the last few moves from both sides have been very natural, this is indeed a critical position.

31...♖ee2?! Black should have paused for 31...♗b7!, a strong move, keeping his options open. The main point is the threat of 32...♖xf3!, which forces White to take on g5. But after 32.hxg5 ♖ee2 White cannot prevent Black from taking on c2, and his best bet would have been running forward with 33.♔b2 ♖xc2+ 34.♔a3 ♖xa2+ 35.♔b4, still keeping minimal chances of an attack against Black's king.

32.♖c3 ♗b7 Here Gelfand had less than a minute left, but with a 10-second increment for every move.

33.♖d1

33...gxh4! 34.♘xf4 ♖e8
Despite his shortage of time, Gelfand comes up with the only way to defend his position.

35.♖h1 ♖c8 36.♖xc8+ ♗xc8

37.♖xh4 At first sight, 37.♘d3!? looks like a better chance, as it keeps more pawns on the board, but after 37...♖xf3 38.♖xh4 ♗f5! Black forces matters, as 39.♔d2 drops the a-pawn after 39...♗xd3 40.cxd3 ♖f2+!, and 39.♖f4 ♖xf4 40.♘xf4 ♔c7 hardly offers any serious winning chances, as White cannot simultaneously handle the black h-pawn and keep his queenside protected.

37...♗f5 38.♖h5
38.♘d3 ♖xf3 transposes to the above.

Special guest on the day of Game 6 was Garry Kasparov. The 13th World Champion gave a press conference, joined the live commentary and played a simul against young talents.

38...♗xc2! Simplest.
39.♖b5+ ♔a8! Not to the c-file, of course, as 40.♖c5+ then wins the bishop.
40.♘d5 a6!
Avoiding mate, and thus almost ending any white hopes of victory.
41.♖a5 ♔b7 42.♘b4 ♗g6 43. ♘xa6 ♖xf3 44.♘c5+ ♔b6 45.b4

This position is a draw, of course, but it is also obviously more pleasant for

White to play. Added to that practical advantage was Vishy's four minutes on the clock against Gelfand's 18 seconds.

45...♖f4 46.a3 ♖g4?!
46...♖f2 would be the cleanest solution, cutting off the white king, with 47.a4 ♔c6! being the point, when Black's king walks to c4.

47.♔d2 h5 48.♘d7+ ♔b7 49. ♘e5 ♖g2+ 50.♔c3 ♗e8 51.♘d3 h4 52.♖e5 ♗g6 53.♘f4 ♖g3+ 54.♔d4 ♗c2

Now Black is almost there, as exchanging a couple of pawns obviously helps the defender.

55.♖h5 ♖xa3 56.♖xh4 ♖g3
Despite its clumsy look, 56...♗a4!?, stopping the pawn from marching forward, seems like the easiest solution.

				Match													TPR	Rapid tiebreak					TPR
				1	2	3	4	5	6	7	8	9	10	11	12			1	2	3	4		
Vishy Anand	IGM	IND	2791	½	½	½	½	½	½	0	1	½	½	½	½	6	2727	½	1	½	½	2½	2822
Boris Gelfand	IGM	ISR	2727	½	½	½	½	½	½	1	0	½	½	½	½	6	2791	½	0	½	½	1½	2704

57.♘d5 ♖g5 58.b5 ♗f5?!

Gelfand keeps making good moves, but fails to find an immediate way to resolve the tension.

Here 58...♗d3! would have instantly forced the draw, using a small tactic to attack the b5-pawn.

59.♖h6 ♗g4 60.♖f6

60.♖h7+ ♔b8 61.♘b4 was a more direct try, but Black defends easily with 61...♗f3!, transferring the bishop to the long diagonal.

60...♗f5 61.♖b6+ ♔a7 62.♖g6 ♗f3 63.♖g7+ ♔b8 64.♘c3 ♗b7 65.♔c4 ♗f3 66.♔b4 ♗d5 67.♘a4

Vishy's attempt is starting to take shape. He wants his king on a5, his knight on c5 and the pawn on b6, setting up mating nets for the black king.

67...♖f7 68.♖g5 ♗f3 69.♘c5 ♔c7 70.♖g6

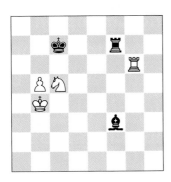

70...♔d8

Logically, Gelfand runs for safety, but

it would actually have been simpler to give White what he wanted.

After 70...♗b7! 71.b6+ ♔b8 72.♖g8+ ♗c8 White has reached his best position, but he has no way to make the slightest progress, as Black has an impregnable fortress.

71.♔a5

71...♖f5??

Played with just under a minute on the clock, and despite being (briefly) the top move of the engines, the losing mistake. 71...♗h1 or something similar holds. Vishy had three minutes left, but took just seconds to play the decisive:

72.♘e6+! ♔c8 73.♘d4! ♖f8 74.♘xf3 ♖xf3 75.♔b6!

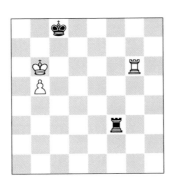

Exploiting the fact that Black's king is on c8, White combines the threat of ♖g8+ with penetration on a7. Black can only defend against one of the threats.

75...♖b3

75...♖f8 would have been the way to draw if the black king had been on b8: 76.♔a7 ♖f7+ 77.♔a8! (77.♔a6 ♖f8 78.♖b6 also wins) 77...♖f1 78.♖a6! ♖b1 79.b6 ♖b2 80.♔a7! Releasing the rook from the defence of the pawn and transferring it to the c-file decides.

76.♖g8+ ♔d7 77.♖b8

And as there is no defence to ♔a7, followed by b6, Gelfand resigned.

The last decisive game in the match, but the adventures were not exactly over. However, Vishy held on to his lead and retained his title, becoming the first player since Lasker to have won World Championship matches against four different opponents.

Quite interestingly, Garry Kasparov was the main critic of Vishy's play in this World Championship match. Interesting in the sense that what Vishy managed to do was to avoid repeating Kasparov's mistakes! Like Vishy, Kasparov won matches in spectacular attacking fashion or by a decisive last-game victory. But facing an opponent who clearly found a strategy to avoid the champion from showing his best, I think Moscow 2012 showed a better approach than London 2000. Not letting your frustration get the better of you, but fighting back. ■

'I understood I was playing with a gun to my head'

While his challenger was drinking in every minute of his first fight for the crown, defending champion Vishy Anand was reliving less uplifting moments. 'It's very difficult to enjoy the World Championship. I think you can enjoy having been in one.' At the end of his longest match since the reunification of the title, the old and new World Champion looks back at a battle that could have gone either way. Contented that he survived and prevailed, but also annoyed at the lack of understanding he was confronted with. 'It's irritating to keep telling people it's not true you're not motivated.'

Dirk Jan ten Geuzendam

The day after he successfully defended his title, all Vishy Anand's time was claimed by a minute-to-minute schedule. Television interviews, calls from home, a lengthy final press conference and an evening reception at the residence of the Indian ambassador to Russia seamlessly followed each other. A good part of the daytime was filled with an unexpected highlight, a visit, together with Boris Gelfand, to Russian president Vladimir Putin in his residence in the woods outside of Moscow.

It's the first thing we talk about when we meet the next day on the seventh floor of the Baltschug Kempinsky Hotel in the suite that served as the 'control room' of his seconds. Dressed in a casual shirt, ditto pants and slip-

said. He spoke a lot with Boris about Belarus and the chess scene.' Anand's eyes sparkle as he recounts a funny part of their conversation. 'I told him that I grew up playing in a chess club which was hosted by the Soviet cultural centre and he said, so you are a problem that we created for ourselves.'

Let's return to the match. What was the predominant feeling the night after the tiebreaks, happiness or relief?

'Simply relief. I have found that in most matches I experience no feelings of happiness. I'm just relieved it's over and relieved that something that could have gone one way went the other way. That's it. I always remember that statement of Euwe's after he became World

you go on obsessing about something, it continues to build up in your head.'

How does this compare to the previous World Championships?

'After it's over you forget how difficult it was very fast. That's a pity, because each time you think, oh my god, was it this bad last time? And Aruna says, yes, it was. In a way it's funny that each match goes a bit further. The Kramnik match finished with Game 11, the Topalov match with Game 12 and now we went for the tiebreaks. The general feeling you have afterwards is just that it is very, very difficult. There's something about playing chess for such high stakes that makes it difficult to relate to anything else. You know this event has this much running on it and

> Anand's eyes sparkle as he recounts a funny part of their conversation
> club which was hosted by the Soviet cultural centre and he said, so you ar

pers, Anand looks relaxed despite an unavoidable lack of sleep in the past few nights. His smile is back, the smile that everyone who knows him well must have missed for much of the past few weeks, when he not only looked concentrated at the board, but also worried, perhaps even unhappy. Talking freely, he offers a drink from the supplies that are still there. Do I want coffee, tea, juice, or perhaps kefir, of which there are still countless bottles in the fridge? I settle for still water and after he has poured some in a coffee cup for me he doesn't bother to look for another glass or cup but takes a swig from the bottle. The visit to Putin has impressed him. 'I thought it was quite an honour, it was a big deal to get an invitation like that. We must have been there for 20 to 30 minutes. He was very warm and friendly. He formally welcomed us for the press, TV and all who were there and then they left the room and he talked. He seemed very well informed about chess. It was very good of you guys to play a match without any conflict, he

Champion. He said, I am supposed to be happy now. Somehow I understand very well what he means. I haven't been happy in these matches, usually just relieved afterwards. Maybe today it's closer to content rather than happy. But I don't feel like doing anything exceptional. Most of the time you just want to be left alone and lie down and spend a few days alone and get used to everything. It's almost a pity that it happens so fast. You're obviously pleased with yourself and then a few days later you think, that is it, I am World Champion. And life goes on. And then you forget about how difficult it was. Now I can still remember how much we suffered and how much tension there was before every game. In general, the only time I was free of tension was when I got to my waiting room some 10 minutes before the start of the game. Then it goes away. You see the board and you think, we start playing. You can stop worrying about what will happen and actually see what will happen. Maybe it's because you have so many months to think about it. If

you understand that your opponent is that much more motivated and he is also really waiting to give all his best.'

I had the feeling that Gelfand was enjoying all this, maybe because it was his first time. Is that a weird feeling if you yourself are not entirely sure that you're enjoying it?

'I don't know. I enjoy it in a certain sense, because it's a fantastic challenge, but while it's happening, you mostly feel the pressure. It's very difficult to enjoy the World Championship. I think you can enjoy having been in one. Maybe it's like running in the morning. Nobody is really happy getting out of bed, but when you get back you go, yeah, it's good that I went for a run. When you've had your shower and get back to the sofa you think, yeah, it was nice that I went out and ran all the way there.'

Were there moments during the match when you felt the title was slipping away from you? Moments of panic?

'Well, quite evidently Game 7 went really badly. During the first six games we had the feeling that both sides were still probing and didn't know what to aim for. After Game 6 I still thought my black opening was holding up well, I wasn't feeling particularly vulnerable with black. But with white we didn't know where to point. And suddenly the match exploded briefly. He won Game 7. It always happens, some area you neglected to pay as much attention to as you should have, and I got into a very bad position. We had seen this position, but when you're not very alert sometimes you miss these things.'

Was it also a much needed wake-up call?
'I don't know. I guess we were already

All's well that ends well. World Champion shares a joke with his seconds Rustam Kasimdzhanov, Radek Wojtaszek and Surya Ganguly at the closing ceremony.

'I told him that I grew up playing in a chess a problem that we created for ourselves.'

getting ready for Game 8 in a big way, but of course it does add a little bit of fire under your backside. Suddenly you feel the intensity much more. You know that the eighth game suddenly matters much more than you thought before. When I got back from Game 7, that was one of the worst days I can remember. I felt so down. I suddenly understood I had five games, but you know this hysterical catching-up mode where you're going on probing against a guy who has so far proven to be almost invulnerable. Then you're trying to probe in a hurry and this and that. These days are washouts normally. I slept badly, from two to five I tossed and turned, then, at six, I just woke up. It was basically awful. So anyway we thought, we'll go for the Grünfeld, we checked the possibility of a King's Indian, we saw this manoeuvre knight e2 to c3, some interesting set-ups, we're gonna do that. I hadn't looked at the specific thing in great detail, but I thought, let's just see what happens. And it's clear that something went slightly wrong with him, because

he missed this queen f2 trick. But in a way the position is already unpleasant. I went king d1 and he took and I took and then I went backstage. And suddenly I saw a move, I couldn't see it clearly, but it seemed to come from the back of the board. And I looked at the monitor and it said queen f6, and I couldn't believe it, and I came back. I was trying to calm down, because basically I knew it was over. So I double-checked once or twice. I had the idea I should check a bit more, but there was nothing to check and I just played it. It must have been a huge disappointment for him that he let me come back, but his demeanour that day clearly suggested that rather than sit on his lead, he was trying to increase it. He wanted a big battle that day. A fairly unusual game, but that's it. In general there are no mistakes in the choices, only in the results.'

Having the same team with which you have been successful before can give you the feeling of re-entering a comfort zone. It may also be a decep-

tive suggestion of strength, based on these previous matches. Did you make, or consider making, any changes?
'It's difficult to see how. The guys like each other a lot, we like each other, we like being together. There is a, well maybe comfort zone is a good word. The problem might be that it may be difficult to come up with new stuff, but I didn't think this was an insolvable problem. And anyway, we did speak to some other people as well.'

During the previous match against Topalov you had some remarkable helpers that were only revealed after the match (Kasparov, Carlsen and Kramnik – DJtG). Will there be any revelations this time?
'This time no real revelations. Garry more or less made it evident he wasn't helping this time (laughs). Magnus didn't help and Vlady also was obviously neutral. When Gelfand quali-

fied, my first thought was, he's much more of an insider than I am. He's had everybody over to his house in Israel. He cooked for them, they cooked for him. He's the ultimate insider. His web of personal contacts is hard to beat.'

Your other helpers were people you might expect from India or from your circle of friends.

'How do you define help? A five-minute chat on Skype, a guy who sends you notes? There are various degrees. It's nice to have lots of friends that you can turn to. Anyone who gives you an idea is useful.'

Before the match you said that no one has to tell you how important a world championship match is. That your entire body automatically reacts to this challenge. Did you have or manage to keep that feeling as the match unfolded?

'I think I managed. First of all, when you have a whole team generating so much work, then only keeping track of everything they are doing gives you that feeling. The output has gone up substantially. And you know you have to execute all that at the board, so you also become more serious and focused. In that sense the world championship will induce some seriousness even if it wasn't there before. It was

also... I'm as unhappy as anyone else with my results of last year. And there is generally nothing to discuss. I have to agree with anyone who criticized my play last year, you can't defend this, these three tournaments. But in December I did not have the luxury of sitting and wallowing in this. I had to start thinking of the match. In a way it's cruel. You know the problem that you want to fix and have to fix and at the same time you know you don't have any time to spend on it and have to move on. So I simply stopped thinking about anything but the match. But still these results left their impact. They hurt your confidence a bit.'

Kasparov thought that you had problems with your motivation. That you were not motivated anymore. That is not what you feel?

'No, I think a lot of people fall in love with a certain narrative and then if your play doesn't match up to that you are not motivated and you're not playing well and blah blah blah. The problem was that they started with the narrative that I am the overwhelming favourite or that I am the favourite. And they come up with some key phrase: Gelfand hasn't beaten Anand since 1993. And then they say that therefore it's obvious that he is playing way below his best. But for me the

match went exactly as expected. Not the specific opening choices he made, and in that he was incredibly good. But even that I had predicted. I had predicted that someone like Boris, who was brought up in the best traditions of the old Soviet Union, he knows how to prepare, he knows how to be a professional. He's spoken to Polugaevsky, he's grown up with all these people, Botvinnik, Kasparov. And on top of that, he impressed me during the entire cycle. In Khanty-Mansiysk and Kazan he showed his determination and focus on something he really wanted to do and achieve. For the rest, well, we both came here with bad tournament records. He was minus five in his last two tournaments, I was 50 per cent in my last three. If you look at my last tournaments and say I was not motivated, you can also say that he was not motivated. It's clear that at some point we both started thinking about the match and we couldn't do anything else. But I didn't see myself as the overwhelming favourite, nor did I think that the match was going to be smooth in any way or that I could impose my will. I knew he would prepare very cleverly, he would sidestep a lot of our opening preparation and then it becomes a kind of endurance contest or a war of attrition. You sit there and play game after game, wait-

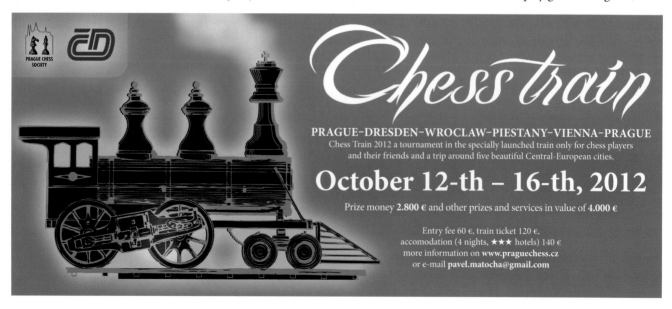

ing for your chances. Boris does this very well, by the way. In all his matches he has shown that he is able to wait and wait for his chance and strike when it comes. With Grischuk, with Mamed, came back quite strongly against Kamsky when the need arose. But also if you look at Khanty-Mansiysk, against Vachier, Ponomariov, I mean, very impressive... It was clear to me that he would be a very difficult opponent. I knew what the title meant to him and what the chance to be here meant to him. I don't think I lacked motivation or lacked anything, it's just that he was very good in controlling the play. He kept on playing unexpected choices. He's never played the Grünfeld before, he's never played ...e6 in the Rossolimo before. Everywhere he tried to find very intelligent choices. With white also. I never got a chance to implement the greater part of my preparation. A lot of it really stayed hidden. He didn't give me a chance and you have to give him credit for that. And the other point: he hasn't beaten me since 1993. But I've only beaten him once since 1997. Our history is quite funny. He won the first four games, then I won in Linares, he won in Biel. Then I won the next four games, in 1996 and '97, I was just beating him everywhere. So he made plus-4 before, I made plus-4 afterwards, we equalized our scores. Afterwards I beat him nine years later and then another six years later we play the match. So this phrase, he hasn't beaten you since 1993, what's the point of that? Since 1997 I have beaten him once.'

The other statistic was that going into the tiebreak you were leading him 8-1 in rapid play.
'Yeah, it's clear that in rapid I had a huge score against him.'

Did that play a role when you decided to offer him a draw in Game 12?
'No, the thing is... First of all, it's true, his last move was a slight mistake, Rook hd8. Perhaps I didn't appreci-

ate it enough, because after Rook ad8 we shook hands immediately. Because the rook is coming to d4, attacking h4, and he will play a4 and leave me with the pawn, and believe me, if I have b3, d3, f3, f2, h4 against his pawns, and four rooks, I am not going to win. He can keep attacking the b- and d-pawns back and forth, he can double on the fourth and attack my h4-pawn, he can double on the b-file and sit there forever. It's zilch. But he played the other rook and I was under the influence of basically already wanting to offer a draw after bishop takes f3, and I thought it came to the same thing. And I thought, let's just finish it and move on. I agree that I could have played a few more moves, but it was a nervous reaction. Maybe it was a lapse of concentration, but I was not aiming for the tiebreaks. The whole thing was, against an opponent who is always patient, who is always willing to be steady, you cannot go like a kamikaze guy. You have to be ready to also go steady and wait for your chance. I was never aiming for the tiebreak, because I generally agree with the opinion that I wasn't a favourite in the tiebreak either. I know my results in rapid chess, but with stakes like this and tension like this it's not your skills at rapid chess that are going to decide the match. Tension plays a bigger role than skill in rapid chess.'

Still, when I was talking to friends of you like Peter Svidler or Vladimir Kramnik during the classical games, they would say, we haven't seen the real Vishy yet. You give the credit for that to Boris.
'That's what I felt. I felt he was not giving me any chance to play and he was very effective in neutralizing me. The thing is, when your previous results haven't been impressive either, you don't know if it's your opponent who is stopping you or if you are in bad form yourself. I will tell you, the first rapid game was the first time I felt very good in the match, because it was the first time I managed to do something

very exciting with the black pieces. After that I realized that the match was opening up and I felt (speaks emphatically) very excited. That was when I really got that feeling back. For the rest he kept me on a tight leash. It's probably a bit of both. Good form, bad form, this is very subjective.'

But then you don't nail that first game and let an advantage slip in the second game. That must have been disconcerting.
'A little bit, but the thing is, we're both good defenders. In Game 2 he defended incredibly well. Even after I hit him with this idea he kept finding resources. The endgame where I am playing two rooks and knight against two rooks and bishop, I thought he played some brilliant moves there. He knows how to make moves that are unpleasant. I don't know if they're the best, they probably are, they're unpleasant and he is very good at this. But it's also important that you're not sitting there thinking, ah, I missed a chance in Game 1 or 2. I just kept waiting and then, in Game 2, he was in severe time-pressure and with a pawn on b5 and a knight floating around it's not at all trivial to draw this. So I thought, I'm entitled to try a bit. I was waiting for a chance and then he went rook f5 and something clicked and I knew I was getting into my rook ending and it was over very quickly. But in fact nothing had been decided yet. In Game 3 he had a completely winning position. In the opening I screwed up badly, but then I saved it.'

Did you spot this one moment on move 26, when he could have won a piece?
'No, I hadn't noticed it.'

But you must have been relieved when he went back with the rook...
'I don't even remember those stages where... Somehow I know we ended up in a position where I was a pawn down, but my knight was active and my pawn chain was fixed and I

thought, with what I had before, this is awesome. But then, I am there and I can make a draw, but I kept missing something and suddenly I was confused about how to take these two pawns under control, one on c6 and one on h3. The beauty is, I had actually been looking at this kind of rook ending before in the match. Every day I looked at some rook endings and I remember I could somehow get a Vancura position. I was optimistic when his king was cut off that I was getting a Vancura position. Which in fact I am not getting. I can just resign. Well, of course it is tragedy, in a position where ♔g3 wins and in a position where 'pass' wins, he made the only move which loses two tempi, which is rook h7, because the rook has to go back

and after a few moves I was just terribly unhappy with my position and I thought I was seriously worse. I felt relieved when he played ...f5. After ...f5 my bishop opens up and I thought, I'll double on the e-file and things will happen. When he went g4, hg, king g4, I thought I'd blundered again, and then I saw knight h2 check. That was the key move. Once that happened, I could start breathing more easily. When I saw bishop g5 check, king g5, king b1, I knew it was over because the rook will sit on e6 forever. The rapid games more or less continued this pattern of both of us being very well matched. In the end almost nothing separated us, but that's it. It seems that my rapid skills did count for something in the end, but you don't want to pin your hopes

after each sentence... You can't think. It would be nice if we could answer questions instead of a lot of the chit-chat. To ask, was it your strategy to make a draw? That I found painful, because it's irritating. People started off with an impression of the match of, ah, Anand is tired and bored, uninterested. He wants to make draws all the time and head for the tie-break. And you find it very patronizing. I mean, I would have been happy for amazing stuff to happen, but Boris wasn't letting me into my preparation. And ditto in reverse. We were probing each other with high stakes. We might have done incredibly exciting things, but we were unable to. And it would have been nice to have some understanding.'

'If one of us had taken an unacceptable risk in one of these Nobody would praise us for taking unacceptable risks.

to h8 and then I just walk back with my king. Of course, this is tragic, but it was an awfully tense game anyway. 'And then Game 4. I knew this was exactly what I should not do, play for a draw. But somehow I was sitting there and I got very tense and I couldn't...'

This was not part of the plan you made with your seconds the day before?
'No, no, no, I hadn't prepared this. I know it's good not to be in two minds, so I decided to go for this bishop b5 check and try to make a draw. But I took on d6 and then went queen e2,

on this. It was still incredibly close.'

Reading your body language, I often had the feeling you were not very happy sitting at the board. This feeling was often strengthened at the press conferences. Sometimes it was so blatantly obvious that you didn't want to be there.
'Yeah. After some games you are still tense and excited. And they keep interrupting you after every sentence, can I translate you now? It really breaks your rhythm. Actually, I was happy to answer the questions the best I could, but if they keep stopping you

You're already feeling frustrated and they are rubbing it in...
'Well, frustrated is too strong a word, because you know it's too easy for every match to go wonderfully and to get all the stuff you want to get in in every match. That strikes me as a bit naïve. But when the undercurrent is always, and I'd been feeling this for a while now, that everybody thinks you are no longer interested in life, that you're just sitting on your ass... You find this patronizing. How many times can you say, no, I'm trying. I remember being very annoyed that by Game 9 they started asking about the tiebreaks.

We were trying. We actually found some new stuff in Game 10, in Game 12. In Game 11 I tried to surprise him. We were probing, but both sides were holding up well. It's irritating to keep telling people it's not true that I wasn't motivated. You've seen these comedy shows where one person says, calm down, don't be excited. (Raising his voice) I am calm!! I am calm!! How many times can you tell somebody that you're calm. You cannot calmly tell someone a hundred times that you're calm. It's just not possible. A lot of people just looked at my recent results and somehow the perception crept in that I didn't care about my results, I didn't care about tournaments, I'm just unmotivated and uninterested. At some point it gets to you. At least

crossed my mind, if I lose here, what will happen? I don't know. I'm gonna play Bazna, I'm gonna play Wijk aan Zee, those are confirmed and I guess the answer would depend. Had I lost the match, that would have been a really heavy blow. That's not to say I am only interested in the world title, but it's the only thing I am still defending. Most of my other records are disappearing. It's not only about the record. I understand that I'll have to play better in the next bunch of tournaments. I want to play better, I'll try to play better, but I don't like to do this with a gun to my head. I mean, if you go to a tournament where you think, well, this time I am really going to try and make an effort, and you have to answer 40 questions about whether

who was playing for survival. I played cautiously, but with great concentration, and I think that on the last day I played some intense games. We made mistakes, but I played intense games. And I felt intense. And like I said, I was very happy with Game 1 of the tiebreak, because I created things with black, things were happening, I really enjoyed that.'

You even forgot about the gun...
'Yes, no, I mean, I am not saying I should be immune to criticism. Every fan passionate about chess is entitled to his or her opinion, of course, but sometimes it gets a bit much. That's why I found these press conferences so disagreeable. Maybe it was because the worst of my last three tournament performances was Tal. That's clear, I mean, it was just hideous. So maybe they got a sense that I was completely gone. I will try to do better, but I think I would like to try it in such a way that I will enjoy a chess tournament again.'

games and lost the match...
They'd say, what an idiot.'

for the match they should understand that I was very motivated. Maybe we were a bit cautious, but Games 11 and 12, what do you expect from us? Especially someone who remembered vividly what happened in Sofia? When one guy crossed the line. By the way, if one of us had taken an unacceptable risk in one of these games and lost the match... Nobody would praise us for taking unacceptable risks. They'd say, what an idiot. And look how brilliantly his opponent punished his irresponsible play. You're not going to get any credit for this. So you have to give it your best shot. It's impossible to answer these questions patiently over and over again. At some point I lost interest in answering their questions.'

What I found remarkable was the number of people speculating about you ending your career in case you'd lose. Do you have any end-of-career plans? Like Kamsky says, the moment I turn 40 I will quit. Have you given that some thought?
'Well, after Game 7 the thought

you're interested in life or when are you going to quit chess, then either you walk out of the press conference or your zest for the tournament goes.'

What you just mentioned I've often thought. You've won everything and I always thought, he can win everything. There's just one thing you should never do, and that's putting that gun to his head. That's the only thing he doesn't like. Is that the negative side of this match, that you had the feeling you were playing with a gun to your head?
'Well, I was! (laughs) This time I understood that I was actually playing with a gun to my head.'

The gun of the outside world...
'The gun of the outside world, the gun of the journalists, that was there. But the main gun was that I understood that I was playing for survival. Now each match in a sense is survival, but given my previous results I understood I was playing for my survival in this match. And I played like someone

The rooms around us, a long row on the side of the hotel that offers a stunning view of Red Square and the Kremlin, are mostly deserted now. Apart from Surya Ganguly, all seconds are gone. Early in the morning the other members of the team, Hans Walter Schmitt and Eric van Reem, have also left. Hotel staff are cleaning the rooms, preparing them for new guests. Anand and his wife Aruna will fly home in the evening. High on his list of priorities is to play with his son Akhil a lot. It's been a long time. 'When I was training I was on Skype with him every day, and Aruna was there. During our stay in Moscow, Aruna spoke to him once or twice, while he was staying with his grandparents. The last day was very cute, because after I won the tiebreak the news reports showed our photos. And then he went to the TV and tried to kiss his mother.' Anand smiles one of his best smiles. 'And when his grandmother told us the story, you can understand how keen we were to catch this flight tonight.' ■

Nakamura
Reclaims Home
Court Title

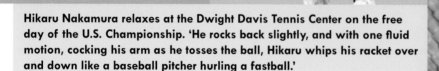

Hikaru Nakamura relaxes at the Dwight Davis Tennis Center on the free day of the U.S. Championship. 'He rocks back slightly, and with one fluid motion, cocking his arm as he tosses the ball, Hikaru whips his racket over and down like a baseball pitcher hurling a fastball.'

PHOTOS MACAULEY PETERSON

Three down, five to go. Hikaru Nakamura returned to his national championship, after a year's absence, as the heavy favorite. He finished a point clear, beating his nearest rival Gata Kamsky with black in the process. Fischer's record eight U.S. titles all came with at least a point margin, and speaking of points, Nakamura is now within three on the Elo scale of Bobby's all time rating peak (not that he's counting)! From St. Louis **Macauley Peterson** has the play-by-play.

A few minutes drive from the Chess Club and Scholastic Center of Saint Louis, in the ample confines of Forest Park, lies the Dwight Davis Tennis Center. Dwight F. Davis was a St. Louis native, and after founding the famous international team tournament now known as the Davis Cup, he served as the

city's parks commissioner, where he created the first municipal tennis courts in the United States. The modern day Davis Center boasts nineteen public courts, and on court six at 11.00 a.m. on the rest day of the U.S. Championship, Hikaru Nakamura is practising his serve.

He rocks back slightly, and with

one fluid motion, cocking his arm as he tosses the ball, Hikaru whips his racket over and down like a baseball pitcher hurling a fastball. It is impressive, albeit marred by a nagging tendency to overshoot the service line. Even so, one gets the impression that with a few slight adjustments, the U.S. number one could be firing aces.

St. Louis has been home to the U.S. Championship since 2009, which was also the last time Nakamura took top honors. Back then the twenty-one year old Hikaru had just broken into the top 30 in the world, and was poised to crack the ranks of elite tournament players.

Now, three years on, the situation is quite a bit different. Nakamura has established himself in the top 10 and has more elite invitations than he knows what to do with. His return to St. Louis this spring was therefore a very welcome development for the organizers, and for fans nationwide.

Nakamura is a prolific player. A glance at his FIDE rating history reveals just one period of inactivity in his entire career to date: May, 2011 was the only time in which he played no rated games. In April last year, he sat out the U.S. Championship despite having moved to St. Louis to become a spokesperson and 'grandmaster advisor' to the Chess Club, in 2010.

At the time, Nakamura's decision, ostensibly to focus on his ultimate quest for the World Championship, was heavily influenced by Garry Kasparov, although it wasn't publicly known until November that they were working together (see New In Chess 2011/7). Hikaru came to regret heeding Kasparov's advice, and regarded the former champion's mentoring style as heavy-handed meddling.

After all, the logic of avoiding weaker opposition ran counter to Nakamura's proclivity to play in a variety of events, including national leagues, and even the occasional open tournament, where diligently pursuing rating points can hardly be seen as the overriding goal. Plus, hadn't Fischer pursued U.S. titles one after the other, all the while compet-

ing in premier international events?

Surprisingly (and file this away in your trivia collection!), Nakamura was one of two players who actually *did not qualify*, and instead had to be invited via an organizer wild card (Seirawan was the other). Despite his being one of the most active of the world's elite grandmasters in 2011, he nevertheless didn't meet the U.S. Championship activity requirement, which dictates that at least eight tournament games (against masters or better) be played *within the United States* over the previous twelve months.

Thirty Love

The early rounds of the championship went more or less smoothly. Nakamura won his first three white games, against Robert Hess, Ray Robson, and Gregory Kaidanov.

Hess and Robson are rising stars, both of whom, Nakamura said in a pre-tournament interview, could compete for the title if they played consistently at their peak.

Hess, whose breakout runner-up performance as a 17-year-old IM in the 2009 Championship surprised many, has seen his rating rise steadily since, but over the past year obligations as a freshman at Yale University have cut into his time. He managed to arrange his schedule to be able to play this year, but had to submit a final term paper the day before the first round.

Robson has been home schooled most of his life, but plans to join the class of 2016 at Webster University, on a chess scholarship, as part of the new Susan Polgar Institute for Chess Excellence (SPICE), that was recently relocated from Texas Tech University.

Ray has grown into a lanky 17-year-old with a modest demeanor, the polar opposite of Nakamura's sometimes irascible bravado. On the tennis court Robson reliably keeps the ball in play,

> ## 'Surprisingly, Nakamura had to be invited via an organizer wild card'

and in their head-to-head, with his long arms and quick feet he managed to outlast Nakamura in a friendly set.

At the chess board in Round 3, however, Nakamura got the best of a wild Yugoslav Dragon Sicilian, culminating in a spectacular king march that earned him the second Best Game prize, as judged by Garry Kasparov.

NOTES BY
Ray Robson

SI 17.3 – B76
Hikaru Nakamura
Ray Robson
St. Louis 2012 (3)

Facing Nakamura for the first time ever was bound to be exciting for me, as he has been a player I have looked up to since I was young.
I had had a bad start with ½/2, so I was hoping to start my comeback with a decent result in this game.
1.e4
This was the first small surprise. Nakamura had already played 1.e4 in his first round, but nowadays he usually chooses not to advance his king's pawn on the first move. I was actually more worried about 1.e4, as I felt I didn't have any solid lines to rely on in this game.
1...c5
The other move I sometimes play is 1...e6, but eventually I decided to go with the Dragon.
2.♘f3 d6 3.d4 cxd4 4.♘xd4 ♘f6 5.♘c3 g6 6.♗e3 ♗g7 7.f3 ♘c6 8.♕d2 0-0 9.g4

Another small surprise. This move seems to have experienced a revival at the top level lately. White simply wants to delay castling and continue with h4, so Black cannot continue normally. 9.g4 also has the benefit of preventing 9...d5 due to 10.g5.

9...♗e6

The other main line is 9...♘xd4 followed by 10...♗e6, but releasing the tension favors White. For example, White cannot continue with h4 here because of ...d5!

10.♘xe6

This is an obvious move, but for a long time it wasn't considered a very good one. Recently some resources have been found for White, and now g4 is usually played in connection with ♘xe6.

10.h4 d5 should be good for Black. 10.0-0-0 ♘xd4 11.♗xd4 ♕a5 was the old main line, which is considered fine for Black.

10...fxe6 11.0-0-0 ♘e5 12.♗e2

12...♕c8

I had actually already had this position against Socko at the Aeroflot Open. He decided to play 12...♗h6,

Ray Robson (seen with Alexander Onischuk): 'Facing Nakamura for the first time ever was bound to be exciting for me, as he has been a player I have looked up to since I was young.'

and eventually won after mistakes by both sides. Hikaru's choice is more critical.

12...♖c8 is another logical move, but after 13.♘b5! White has been doing well.

13.h4 ♘fd7

Black may or may not want to take the f3-pawn. The main idea is just stopping ♗h6.

13...♘c4 14.♗xc4 ♕xc4 15.♗h6 is slightly better for White.

14.f4

14.h5 was still possible, since 14...♘xf3!? 15.♘d5! is a nice blow (14...♘c4 is also possible, and after 15.♗xc4 ♕xc4 16.hxg6 hxg6 the position isn't completely clear, since Black can often run with his king to the center if necessary). I had thought

this was better for White, but Black seems to get a reasonable position in any case:

ANALYSIS DIAGRAM

15...♘xd2 (15...exd5 16.♕xd5+ ♖f7 – 16...♔h8? 17.hxg6 ♘f6 18. ♖xh7+ ♘xh7 19.♕h5 and Black gets mated or loses too many pieces – 17.♗xf3 with a slight white advantage) 16.♘xe7+ ♔f7 17.♘xc8 ♖axc8 18.♖xd2 ♔e7 (Black shouldn't really have problems due to his dark-square control) 19.hxg6 hxg6 20. ♗g5+ ♔f6!? 21.♖h7+ ♖f7 22.♗xf6+ ♔xf6 23.g5+ ♔e7 24.♖xf7+ ♔xf7 25.♖xd6 ♘e5, and Black has good compensation.

14...♘c4 15.♗xc4 ♕xc4 16.e5

I knew I had seen this position before,

but unfortunately I didn't remember the right way.

The Saint Louis Chess Club has become the home of the U.S. Championships.

16...♘b6? 16...♖ad8 is probably the best move, when the position is still unclear. **17.h5** Now White gets a big and easy attack.
17...dxe5 18.hxg6 hxg6 19.♕h2

19...♖xf4 Unfortunately the only move. 19...exf4 20.♗d4 is simply crushing for White. **20.♗xf4** 20.♔b1 ♘d5! is good for Black.

20...♕xf4+ 21.♔b1 I had actually completely missed this when I took on f4. For some reason I thought he was forced to exchange queens.
21...♕xh2 22.♖xh2 ♖f8

Still, the position isn't as bad as it looks for Black. I am quickly getting some counterplay with ...♖f4, and if

I eventually activate my bishop with ...e4 I will have counterplay.
23.♘e4
The computer recommends 23.b3 ♖f4 24.♘e2, with the idea of 24...♖xg4 25. ♖d8+ ♔f7 26.♖b8, when the knight on e2 is doing a good job preventing Black from getting counterplay.
23...♖f4

24.♘g5?

It made more sense to go to c5 and take the b7-pawn. The pawn on e6 isn't completely useless, but the one on b7 looks much tastier. After 24. ♘c5 ♖xg4 25.♘xb7 White has decent chances of winning.

24...♖xg4 25.♘xe6 ♗f6

I wasn't sure whether or not I should be afraid of ♘xg7. The bishop could be a strong piece in the future, though, so I think ...♗f6 makes sense.

26.b3

Now White just wants to play c4, when my knight will have major issues. Therefore:

26...♘c8

27.c4

27.♖d8+ ♔f7 28.♘c5 ♘d6 29.♖h7+ ♗g7 doesn't give White anything.

27.♖f2!? was an interesting try to prevent Black's knight from getting into the game; after 27...b6 (27...♘d6? 28. ♖xd6) 28.c4 ♔f7 29.♘c7 e4 Black still has good chances of saving the game.

27...♘d6 28.c5 ♘b5 29.♖d7

I was in time-trouble at this point, so Hikaru was playing quite quickly. I should mention that Hikaru played the whole game while hardly consuming any time.

29...♔f7

I had thought this was a mistake, but now I think that 37...♖e1+ was the decisive error.

29...e4! was probably also good enough to hold: 30.♖xb7 ♖g1+ 31.♔c2 ♖a1!.

ANALYSIS DIAGRAM

This is the whole point. Now 32. ♖xb5 looks critical, which leads to an amazing line: after 32...♖xa2+ 33.♔c1 ♖xh2 34.c6 e3 35.c7 ♖h1+ 36.♔c2 e2 37.c8♕+ ♔h7 38.♘f8+ ♔g7 (38...♔h6?? fails to 39.♕e8 ♖g1 40.♘f7) 39.♘e6+ (after 39.♕e8 Black can escape to h8, and after 39... e1♕ 40.♕xg6+ ♔h8 41.♖h5+ ♖xh5 42.♕xh5+ ♔g7 he actually wins) 39...♔h7

ANALYSIS DIAGRAM

40.♖e5 (40.♖b8 ♖c1+! – 40...e1♕?? 41.♕g8+ ♔h6 42.♕h8+! ♗xh8 43. ♖xh8 mate – 41.♔xc1 e1♕+ 42.♔c2 ♕e2+, with a perpetual) 40...♖xe5 41.♕f8 (41.♘g5+ ♔g7 42.♘f3 e1♕ (42...e1♘+!?) 43.♘xe1 ♖xe1 44.♕d7 ♗d6 45.♕xa7 ♖e4, and it will end as a draw) 41...♗f6 42.♕f7+ ♔h6 43. ♘f8 e1♘+ (somehow Black makes every move with check, and so he can

survive) 44.♔d2 ♘f3+ 45.♔e2 ♘h4, and Black guards g6 while protecting the rook from ♕h7+.

30.♖xb7 The following sequence of moves seems forced.

30...♖g1+ 31.♔c2 ♘a3+ 32.♔b2 ♘b1 33.♘d8+ ♔e8 34.♘c6 e4+ 35.♔c2 ♘a3+ 36.♔d2 ♘b1+ 37.♔e3

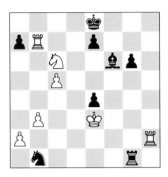

37...♖e1+?

This check only helps White's position. The right move was 37...♘c3!, when Black's pieces are all coordinating well. The knight does several things well here. First of all, it discourages any immediate captures on e7 due to ♘d5+ forks. Also, after the black rook gives a few checks, the knight will either help support the advance of the pawn to e2 or go back to d5, where it supports e7 and prepares an e4-e3 advance: 38.♖xa7 (38.♖h7? ♖g3+ 39.♔f2 ♖f3+ 40.♔g1 ♘d5 shows the great activity of the black pieces. Black may already start playing to win here) 38...♖d1 39.♔f2 ♖d3!? (White should probably just force a draw here)

ANALYSIS DIAGRAM

40.♖h7 e3+ 41.♔g2 e2 42.♖hxe7+ ♗xe7 43.♖xe7+ ♔f8 44.♔f2 ♖h3

(44...♖d1 45.♖xe2 ♘xe2 46.♔xe2 is also a simple draw) 45.♔e1 ♘xa2 46. ♖xe2 ♘c1 47.♖f2+ ♔e8, and all the pawns come off the board.

38.♔f2 ♖c1 39.♖h7 ♖c2+

40.♔g3?

Hikaru played this practically instantly, but this could have thrown the win away.

Instead, 40.♔e3 was the right move. After 40...♘c3 41.♔e5! Black is completely lost: 41...♖d1+ 42.♔f4 ♖f2+ 43.♔g4 ♘e3+ 44.♔h3 and White wins.

40...♖c3+?

Unfortunately I was playing on the increment here, and at the last second I made this stupid move.

I should have played 40...♘c3! (the key point is that ♘xe7 isn't a threat due to ...♗e5+, and so I can just bring my knight back into play) 41.♖hxe7+ (probably best – after 41.♖xa7 ♘d5 Black is not in any danger, and so White should try to find a draw) 41... ♗xe7 42.♖xe7+ ♔f8 43.♖xa7 ♘e2+ (43...♘xa2 should also draw, but 43...♘e2+ is simpler) 44.♔g4 ♘c3!, and Black has enough counterplay to draw, for instance: 45.♘e5 ♖g3+

46.♔h4 g5+ 47.♔h5 ♘f4+ 48.♔h6 e3 49.♖a4 e2 50.♖e4 ♖g1 51.♘f3 ♖f1 52.♔xg5 ♖xf3 53.c6 ♘d5 54.♖xe2.

41.♔g4

Now I realized that I was completely

> 'When I saw Hikaru hovering his hand above the knight I got excited, and then he played it!'

lost. I couldn't find any reasonable moves, but I didn't want to resign and so played:

41...e3 42.♘xe7 e2

Here I was expecting a normal continuation like 43.♖b8+, when White will stop the pawn on e2 and win easily. When I saw Hikaru hovering his hand above the knight I got excited, and then he played it!

43.♘d5!!

Two exclams just for the idea. 43.♖b8+ ♔d7 44.♘xg6+ ♔c6 45.♖e8 and White wins.

43...♖g3+ 44.♔f4 ♗g5+

I had seen that 44...♗e5+ would lose

to 45.♔xe5 followed by 46.♔d6, but I somehow didn't imagine that it could work with the bishop on the board.

45.♔e5 e1♕+ 46.♔d6

A great position. Black has an extra queen, but is completely lost against the threats of ♖h8+ and ♖b8+.

46...♗f4+

Or 46...♖f3 47.♖b8+ ♗d8 48.♘c7+, and Black gets mated.

47.♘xf4 ♖d3+

Or 47...♕d2+ 48.♘d5, and the knight comes back and guards everything.

48.♘xd3 ♕g3+ 49.♘e5

Again the knight dominates the queen. Here I resigned.

■ ■ ■

Thirty Thirty

With black, Nakamura drew against third seed Alexander Onischuk and 'dark horse' contender Alejandro Ramirez. Onischuk is a perennial top finisher, and the only other American player (after Nakamura and Kamsky) in the world's top 100, but after losing to Kamsky in Round 3 he was never in a position to challenge for the title.

Nakamura held the advantage in both middlegames, but was unable to convert, a problem he cites as a lingering weakness in his game. Hikaru calls the draw with Ramirez 'a very big disappointment'. Indeed, it was a game that GM Ben Finegold and WGM Jennifer Shahade, hosting the live commentary webcast, had essentially stopped following, presuming that Nakamura would go on to win easily, once this position appeared on the board:

Ramirez-Nakamura
Round 2
position after 35.♕c1

In this critical position, Nakamura played: **35...♚f7**
Instead, after 35...♚h7 Ramirez was going to play 36.♗xh6, which loses to a spectacular pawn sacrifice: 36...♕f3 37.♗e3 (37.♕e3 ♕xe3 38.♗xe3 is a hopeless endgame for White) 37...f4!

ANALYSIS DIAGRAM

(gaining the h6-square for his king – 37...♖d1 38.♕c7+ only leads to perpetual check) 38.gxf4 ♖d1 39.♕c7+ ♚h6 40.f5+ g5, and White runs out of moves.
36.♗xh6 ♕f3 37.♕c5
And Ramirez escaped with a draw.
37...♚e6 38.♗e3 a6 39.♕c8 ♕d5 40.♕g8+ ♚f6
Draw.
Nakamura had seen a similar line involving the f4-pawn sacrifice, but in a position with his king on f7, when White can still manage a perpetual. 'It was very upsetting,' he said after the championship, 'mainly because in a tournament like this (...) every half point that you have the chance to get – every game you can win – is very important.'

Over on the grandstand

Across the street at the World Chess Hall of Fame, there's also a new king in town. The world's largest chess piece – sanctioned by Guinness – was unveiled (in the rain) at a ceremony just prior to the start of the U.S. Championship. Standing nearly 4.5 meters tall and weighing over a tonne, the plywood king is an ostentatious landmark for the ambitious new museum. 'King Kong', as it was quickly dubbed, is already a popular spot to pose for photos, and even has its own Twitter stream (@STLChessKing).

Inside the Hall of Fame, two new exhibitions provided Championshipgoers with an artful distraction from the grandmaster games going on across Maryland Avenue.

Bobby Fischer: Icon Among Icons, is a stunning collection of photos by Harry Benson (no stranger to New In Chess readers), largely, but not exclusively, dedicated to his time spent with Fischer leading up to and during the 1972 match.

On the ground floor, peculiarly anthropomorphized chess figures spin gently on mechanized pedestals, flanked by a mishmash of sketches and supporting documents related to a new fourteen-minute video projection called 'A Game of Chess', by Marcel Dzama. The surrealist black and white production references several artists from the 1920s and 30s, including the films of Luis Buñuel, and includes a chess game liberally in its narrative. Detail-minded chess players will notice incongruities on the board that go beyond the dreamlogic of the piece, but that's hardly the point.

These investigations into the rich nature of the game and its myriad artistic crossovers are a worthy endeavor and a marvelous complement to the St. Louis chess scene. ∎

STUDIO 314

STUDIO 314

After six rounds of play, Nakamura nevertheless had a half point edge over his main rival Gata Kamsky, thanks in part to a nice victory by Gregory Kaidanov over Kamsky. Kaidanov has played in a whopping seventeen U.S. Championships since immigrating to Lexington, Kentucky, in 1991, but has never won.

NOTES BY
Gregory Kaidanov

SL 3.1 – D15
Gregory Kaidanov
Gata Kamsky
St. Louis 2012 (4)

1.d4 d5 2.c4 c6 3.♘f3 ♘f6 4.♘c3 a6 5.e3 g6
Gata consistently plays this line with very good results. After studying his games I realized that I should try to stay away from c4-c5, because his understanding of those positions greatly exceeds mine.
6.♕b3 ♗g7 7.♘e5 0-0 8.♗e2
A rare system, which previously was tried in only two games. Gata took his time here and played a new move.

8...dxc4
8...e6 9.0-0 ♘bd7 10.f4 was my preparation.
9.♗xc4 e6 Black plans on eventually playing ...b5, ...c5 or both.
10.0-0 ♕c7
The immediate 10...c5 runs into 11. dxc5 ♕c7 12.♘d3 ♘bd7 13.♘a4 ♘e4?! 14.♗xe6, and White maintains his extra pawn.

11.♗e2! A typical move for these positions. White moves his bishop away in anticipation of ...b5, plans a later transfer to f3 and at the same time frees the c4-square for either the queen or a knight.
11...♘bd7
I was going to meet 11...c5 with 12. ♘a4 cxd4 13.♘b6 ♕xe5 14.♘xa8, however, the computer shows that Black has good compensation after 14...b5. In addition, Black also has 12...♘d5!, so maybe 11...c5 is not bad at all.
12.f4 c5 13.♗f3 ♖b8 14.a4
At this point I was very happy with my position.

14...b5!?
14...cxd4 15.exd4 ♕d6 runs into 16. ♘c4 ♕xd4+ 17.♗e3, and although the queen escapes after 17...♕d3 18. ♖ad1 ♕f5, White's position is much better after something like 19.a5.
14...b5 is a very interesting move, connected to a pawn sacrifice.
15.axb5
15.♘c6!? deserved attention: 15...cxd4 (after 15...♖b6 16.axb5 or 15...bxa4 16.♕c2 ♖b6 17.♘e7+ ♔h8 18.♘xa4 White is better) 16.♘xb8 dxc3 17.

♘xd7 ♗xd7 18.♕xc3 ♕xc3 19.bxc3 ♘d5 20.♗xd5 exd5 21.axb5 ♗xb5 22.♖f2 ♖e8!, and Black has some compensation for the exchange, but whether this is enough is hard to tell.

15...♗b7?
As Gata acknowledged after the game, he forgot to insert the exchange on d4. 15...cxd4 16.exd4 ♗b7 17.♗xb7 ♕xb7 18.♖a5 axb5 19.♖xb5 ♕c7 would lead to a position in which Black would have good compensation for the pawn. Both the d4- and the b2-pawns are weak, the bishop on c1 is bad and Black has a Benko Gambit type of play on the open b- and c-files.
16.♗xb7 ♕xb7 17.dxc5! ♘xc5

18.♕a3
In the postmortem Gata criticized this move. He thought that 18.♕c4 was virtually winning. I have to admit that I rejected it on the basis of 18...♖fc8 19.bxa6 ♕a7 after which the opposition of my queen and his rook on the c-file looks unpleasant. However, after 20.♘b5 ♕b6 21.a7 ♖a8 22.b4! White indeed seems to be winning. I still believe it was not easy to see this during the game.
18...♖fc8 19.bxa6 ♕a7

Despite his two extra pawns White's task is not easy. His lack of development and the activity of Black's pieces make the consolidation process difficult. Here I realized that I needed to give up the b-pawn in order to consolidate.

20.b4! ♘cd7 21.♖a2!

21...♗f8 21...♘xe5 22.fxe5 ♘g4 23. ♘e4 ♗xe5 24.h3 ♖c4 25.♕d3 is what I calculated during the game.

22.♘xd7 ♘xd7 23.♘e4 ♖xb4 24.♕d3

White finally untangled his pieces, and thanks to a powerful extra pawn on a6 he has a big advantage.

24...♗g7 25.♗d2 ♖bb8 26.♖b1

White's goal is to trade as many pieces as possible.

26...♘b6 27.♘d6 ♖d8 28.♘b5 ♕a8 29.♕e2 ♘d5 30.a7 ♖bc8 31.♖c1

31...♗f8! Bringing the bishop to c5. At this point we both started getting into time-trouble.

32.♖xc8 ♖xc8 33.h3 h5 34.♔h2 h4 35.e4 ♘f6 36.♖a4 ♘h5

37.♖c4

37.♕d3 was stronger and simpler, but in time-trouble I kept looking for forcing moves, hoping to simplify the position.

37...♖c5 A quite unpleasant move to face in time-trouble.

White would win easily after 37...♘g3 38.♖xc8 ♕xc8 39.♕d3 ♗c5 40.♗c3.

38.♖xc5 ♗xc5

At this point I almost panicked because ...♗xa7 is hard to stop, but luckily the tactics work in my favor.

39.♗e3! ♗xa7

39...♘g3 loses to 40.♗xc5 ♘xe2 41. ♘c7 ♕xe4 42.a8♕+ ♕xa8 43.♘xa8 ♘xf4 44.♗e7.

After 39...♕xe4 White has multiple wins. I saw 40.♘c3, and 40.♗xc5 (40...♕xf4+ 41.♔g1 ♕c1+ 42.♕f1 ♕xc5+ 43.♕f2) is winning too.

40.♗xa7 ♘xf4 41.♕f3 g5 42. ♗e3 ♘g6 43.♘d6 ♕f8 44.♕d1 f6 45.♕d4 ♕b8 46.♕b6 ♕xb6 47. ♗xb6 ♔f8 48.♗d8

Black resigned.

Deuce

Heading into the second half, Nakamura's consecutive draws with Varuzhan Akobian and Yuri Shulman allowed Kamsky to catch up with him, and by Round 8 the two had opened up a point and a half lead over the rest of the field.

Akobian is still looking for his first U.S. Championship title after nine tries, and this year he brought a high-powered second – his friend Gabriel Sargissian. Sargissian previously visited St. Louis for the 2009 Championship when Akobian finished in a solid tie for fourth alongside Kamsky. Akobian's performance this year was good enough to leapfrog into a board spot on the U.S. Olympiad team in Istanbul. After assisting the U.S. team as a coach in several events, the chance to play will be a welcome change for Var.

Shulman won the championship in 2008, when Nakamura and Kamsky both were absent, and he was the runner up to Kamsky for the latter's back-to-back titles in 2010 and 2011. This year Shulman was the only player other than Nakamura to be undefeated. Still, with Yuri's wife WIM Viktorija Ni playing in the Woman's Championship, and their one-year-old son Gabriel (who was born during the 2011 championship) in tow,

Last year Yuri Shulman (l.) came to St. Louis alone, as his wife, WIM Viktorija Ni, stayed at home to give birth to their son Gabriel. Greg Kaidanov happily joins the family photo.

he finished in the middle of the cross-table with only one win to his credit.

The ninth round looked to be an important turning point. Nakamura, playing white with Aleksandr Lenderman, tried for nearly six hours and 121 moves to maneuver his way to a win. He describes the game as 'very brutal, mainly because of the emotional swings', as his evaluation of his own winning chances ebbed.

For a time, there was a very real possibility that, despite a board full of pieces, the game might conclude in a draw by the 50-move rule. Nakamura

marched his king from b1 to g1, while Lenderman could only shuffle his between a7 and b8, with neither side prepared to execute his one break in the position. Afterwards, Nakamura said, half jokingly, that if he'd known about the 166-move record for the longest game in U.S. Championship history, he might have found a moment to start shuffling his pieces again.

When the position finally did open up, neither player had any real winning chances. 'It was very disappointing considering that Gata had won his game three hours earlier', he said.

Advantage Kamsky

Kamsky's win over Yasser Seirawan was remarkable in that up until almost the last move it was all opening preparation he had originally concocted for his 2011 Candidates' match with Veselin Topalov in Kazan.

Kamsky played the entire game at breakneck speed, including the flashy combination that would earn him the $1,500 Best Game prize from Kasparov.

Kamsky-Seirawan
Round 9
position after 21.♘e5

21...♗xc5 22.♗xh6! gxh6 23. ♖d7! 'In the words of my trainer, Nikolay Minev, I'm going to die with a full stomach here', Seirawan said after the game.
23...♕xd7
After 23...♘xd7 24.♕d2 ♔h7 the deft retreat 25.♘g4 is the crusher. 'It's not just checkmate, it's *double*-checkmate', Yasser observed after the game with a chuckle.
24.♘xd7 ♘xd7 25.♕d2
And Black is busted.

Kamsky himself does not consider this game worthy of any great praise. In the post-game chat on the live webcast he explained that the tactical sequence was *entirely* the creation of an engine. 'I remember when I was looking at this line, I also couldn't understand why 21...♗xc5 was bad, and then the computer showed me this (...) I didn't see [♘g4] until the very last moment.'

Yasser Seirawan: 'In the words of my trainer, Nikolay Minev, I'm going to die with a full stomach here.'

At the closing ceremony, just before the Best Game was announced, Gata was even more blunt. 'It has nothing really to do with chess (...) It used to be just a game of intelligent people, they play against each other and it was just pure chess: Who is strong on the board? But right now chess, as you can see from the matches for the world championship, it becomes more and more of a team effort. Basically your whole team is studying for a year. The seclusion, all they do is chess chess chess, analyse lines, prepare. And then the candidates, both of them – the opponents – all they have to do is simply memorize those preparations, get to the board and just show that preparation. There is no chess skill involved in that! It's just all memory and that's it.'

Chess or not, the win put Kamsky in the competitive driver's seat, with two rounds to play, a half point lead, and white against Nakamura next.

Nakamura was in a predicament. 'Originally, I suppose, after the Lenderman game I was in a horrible mood and I was just planning to go completely insane.' That night, he even Tweeted his frustration: 'Time to go on a massive bender in St. Louis!!'

Only the counsel of his trusty sec-

ond Kris Littlejohn restored Hikaru's confidence. 'He was able to sort of reason everything out with me and I just decided to play something solid in the Najdorf, and it was definitely the right decision', Nakamura explained. 'It's a must-win game (...) But I think that's what makes chess great. In these must-win situations I actually feel more excited about playing, because there's more pressure there's more excitement.'

Kamsky changed his mind about what to play against Nakamura just an hour before the game. At the board he couldn't remember what he had prepared, and ended up spending a great deal of time in the opening.

NOTES BY
Hikaru Nakamura

SI 14.5 – B90
Gata Kamsky
Hikaru Nakamura
St. Louis 2012 (10)

1.e4 c5
The best opening move, according to a former world champion. How can one go wrong!
2.♘f3 d6 3.d4 cxd4 4.♘xd4 ♘f6 5.♘c3 a6
In our last encounter in Wijk aan Zee, I tried the Sicilian Dragon. Despite obtaining an advantage, I was unable to break through, and the game was drawn. In this situation, I felt like playing something which kept more pieces on the board.
6.a4

The first surprise of the game. I had looked at a wide variety of possibilities, but I was surprised that Gata went back to this minor sideline, as he did not have a lot of success with it against Topalov in their match.

6...e5 7.♘f3 ♗e7 8.♗c4 0-0 9.0-0 ♗e6

10.♗b3!? An interesting choice by Gata. He played it pretty quickly, so I think it is safe to assume he had prepared it before the game. However, I do not expect this move to become cutting edge theory in the future.

After 10.♕e2 ♕c7 11.♗b3 ♖c8 12. ♗g5 ♘bd7 13.♖fd1 h6 14.♗xf6 ♘xf6 15.♘h4 ♕d7 16.g3 ♖c5 17.♖d3 ♖ac8 Black had complete equality in Ponomariov-Bruzon, Khanty-Mansiysk 2011.

10...♘c6 11.♗g5

11...♘a5!?
The first deviation from theory. At the board I remembered that in some other Najdorf lines with this structure (6.♗e3 e5 7.♘f3) Black can go for this same idea with ...♘c6-a5. It is usually less effective, since White has not played a4, but it seemed like the logical continuation during the game.

After 11...h6 12.♗xf6 ♗xf6 13.♘d5 ♗xd5 14.♗xd5 ♕c7 15.♖a3 White has a small but lasting edge, as was seen in Areschenko-Srinath, New Delhi 2011.

12.♗xf6 ♗xf6

13.♘d5?!
This move is probably not dubious per se, but considering the situation in the tournament, I assumed that having failed to get an advantage out of the opening, Gata would attempt to lock it down.

After 13.♘d5 ♖c8 14.♕d3 ♘xb3 15. cxb3 ♗xd5 16.♕xd5 ♖c6 the position is completely balanced. However, considering this was a must-win game for me, I think this would have been a much more prudent choice.

13...♖c8 14.♘d2
After 14.♕d3 ♘b6 15.♖ab1 ♕b4 16.♘d2 ♖fd8 17.♖fd1 Black is still marginally better, but White has obtained a much better version of the game, as the queen on d3 has access to many more important squares and targets.

14...♕c7 15.♖e1 ♗g5 16.♘f1 ♕b6 17.♖b1 ♘c4 18.♕e2

18...♗h6?!

A tough decision. After 18...h6 19.g3 ♖fe8 20.h4 ♗d8 21.♖ed1 White is completely fine and might be able to fight for the initiative shortly.

In retrospect, 18...g6 19.g3 h5 would have been a better try, as the bishop will have many more squares.

19.h4 ♕b4 20.g3 ♖c7 21.♔g2 ♘b6 22.♗b3 ♗xb3 23.cxb3 ♕xb3 24.a5

24...♘a4?
A bad blunder on my part. However, it is not clear to see why without the aid of the silicon machine. As usual, it continues to laugh endlessly at our feeble abilities to play chess precisely. A messy and complicated position is reached after 24...♘c8 25.♖bd1 ♖c5 26.♘h2 ♕e6 27.♘d5 ♖xa5 28.♘g4, where White has ample compensation for the two sacrificed pawns.

25.♘h2?! Better was 25.♘d5 ♖c5 (White has a substantial advantage heading into the endgame: 25... ♖c2 26.♕d1 ♘xb2 27.♘e7+ ♔h8 28.♕xd6 ♘c4 29.♘f5 ♔g8 30.♘1e3! ♗xe3 31.♖xe3 ♖e8 32.♕a3 ♕a4 33.♕xa4 ♘xa4 34.♖xb7) 26.♘e7+ ♔h8 27.♘f5 d5 28.exd5 ♕xd5+ 29.♔g1 ♕c6 30.♖bd1, and now:

ANALYSIS DIAGRAM

A) 30...f6 31.♘xh6 gxh6 32.♕d2 f5 33.b4 gives a complete mess, but it is easier for White to play;

B) After 30...♖xa5 31.♕g4 e4 32.♘xh6 gxh6 (32...♖xh6 33.♕xe4 ♔g8 34.♖d8! g6 35.♕b4! and White is winning due to the completely misplaced knight and rook on the edge of the board, which are extremely grim) 33.♕f4 White has a crushing attack as well, due to the open king and all of the misplaced pieces on the queenside.

25...g6!?

I spent a lot of time calculating 25...♘xc3, but I could not come up with any advantage in the following line: 26.bxc3 ♕xc3 27.♘g4 ♕d2 (after 27...♕xa5 28.♖ed1 ♕a3 29.♘xh6+ gxh6 30.♖b6 White should be absolutely fine, due to Black's horrible pawn structure and open king) 28.♕d1 ♖fc8 29.♖b6

ANALYSIS DIAGRAM

I am up two pawns here, but with a dead bishop on h6 and a permanent weakness on d6, I suspect White has more than enough compensation.

26.♘g4 ♗g7 27.♕d5 ♖c2 28.♕e3 ♘c5 29.h5 ♕xe3 30.♘gxe3 ♖d2 31.♘c4 ♖d4 32.♘xd6 ♖d8 33.b4

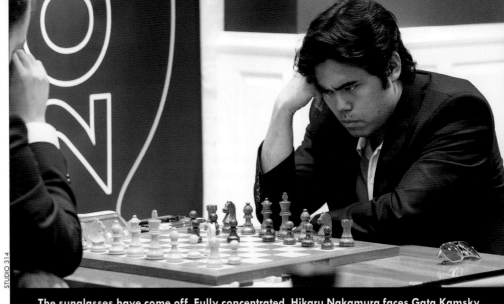

The sunglasses have come off. Fully concentrated, Hikaru Nakamura faces Gata Kamsky.

♘d3 34.♘xb7 ♘xe1+ 35.♖xe1 ♖a8

36.f3?! The first of several crucial mistakes by Gata in time-pressure. White should be able to draw without too much difficulty after 36.♘c5 ♗f8 37.♖h1! h6 38.hxg6 fxg6 39.♘e6 ♖xe4 40.♘f6+ ♔f7 41.♖xe4 ♔xe6 42.♖c1!.

36...♗f8 37.♖c1 ♗xb4 38.♖c7 gxh5

39.♔h3? Black is definitely better after 39.♘xb4 ♖xb4 40.♖d6 f6 41.♔f5 ♔h8 42.♘d6, but I am pretty sure that White can draw this with precise play.

39...♔g7

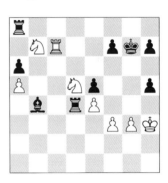

40.♔h4?

The final blunder, after which there is no chance of saving the game.

40.♘xb4 ♖xb4 41.♘d6 ♔f6 42.♖c6 (42.♘xf7 ♖a4 43.♘d6 ♖xa5 44.♖xh7 ♖a3, and Black is winning due to the unstoppable a-pawn in the long run) 42...♖b1 43.♘c4+ ♔g7 44.♘xe5 ♖h1+ 45.♔g2 ♖a1 46.♖c7 ♔f8 47.f4 ♖xa5 48.♘d7 ♖a8 and once again, Black has a big advantage due to the passed a-pawn.

40...♖a7 41.♔xh5 ♖xd5! 42.exd5 ♗xa5 43.♖e7 ♗b6 44.d6 a5

All moves are now losing, since the a-pawn is a freight train which cannot be stopped.

45.♔g5

Instead, 45.d7 ♔f6 46.♖e8 ♖xb7 47. d8♕+ ♗xd8 48.♖xd8 ♖a7 49.♖d3 a4 50.♖a3 e4 51.fxe4 ♔e5 52.♔h6 f6 53. g4 ♔xe4 54.g5 fxg5 55.♔xg5 ♔d4 is a routine endgame win.

Alternatively, 45.♘d8 is met by 45... ♔f8! and now:

ANALYSIS DIAGRAM

A) 46.♘c6 ♖xe7 47.dxe7+ ♔e8 48. ♘xe5 a4 49.♘c4 ♗c5 50.♔h6 ♔xe7 51.♔xh7 ♔e6 52.♔g8 ♔d5 53.♘d2 ♔d4 54.♔xf7 ♔d3 55.♘e4 ♗d4, winning;

B) 46.♖xa7 ♗xa7 47.♘c6 ♗b6 48.♘xe5 a4! 49.♘c4 (49.♘d7+ ♔e8 50.♘xb6 a3) 49...♗c5 50.d7 ♔e7 51.♔h6 ♔xd7 52.♔xh7 ♔e6 53.♔g8 ♔d5 54.♘d2 ♔d4 55.♔xf7 ♔d3 56. ♘e4 ♗d4, winning.

45...a4 46.♔f5 a3 47.♘d8 a2 48.♘e6+ ♔h6 49.♘g5 a1♕ 50. ♘xf7+ ♔g7

Here Gata resigned, as it is hopeless to play on down a queen.

Gata and I both made some errors in the middlegame, but this was an exciting game for the players and spectators alike. This is what we, as professional chess players, should strive for.

■ ■ ■

Kamsky was upset by his lackluster calculation. 'You know, I really didn't like the quality of my games, because I realized that I don't see a lot at the board. I just managed to trust my intuition because I have a huge experience, I've been playing chess for many years at the top level, and I've been relying on intuition to make some choices in my games. But you're not supposed to do that, you're supposed to back up intuition with calculation and preparation.'

Advantage Nakamura

After this critical win, Nakamura was in the clear lead. In his post-game chat on the live webcast, a question came in from the online audience about whether Hikaru would play for a win in the final round, or be content with a draw, figuring that even if Kamsky should also win, Nakamura would still be the favorite in a rapid play-off. 'That's a stupid question,' Hikaru retorted, 'I have white and I'm playing Yasser, and I have a chance to win the tournament, so I might as well just give it my all.'

Calling your fans 'stupid' is not exactly endearing, but then again maybe this bald-faced, take-no-prisoners attitude is what makes him a great player. In any case, it doesn't particularly bother Hikaru.

'At this point in my life, having been a chess professional for many years now (...) There are going to be people who dislike you, and frankly I'm going to do what I have to do. As long as I perform at the board, I think everything else should be secondary.'

So, it was business as usual in Round 11.

FR 1.1 – C00
Hikaru Nakamura
Yasser Seirawan
St. Louis 2012 (11)

1.e4 e6 2.f4

'This tournament was a tournament of many firsts for me, and 2.f4 was a first', Seirawan said on the live webcast.
2...d5 3.e5 c5 4.♘f3 ♘c6 5.c3 ♘ge7 6.♘a3 ♘f5 7.♘c2 h5

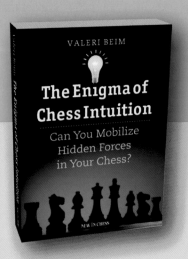

7...d4 was Stripunsky-Nakamura, 2010 U.S. Championship, a game Hikaru won and remembered.

8.♗d3 'The only move which really makes a lot of sense.'
8...g6 9.0-0 ♗e7

10.♗xf5 gxf5
But this was a surprise. In retrospect both players agreed that this may already be the losing move, and that Black should go for a solid ...exf5, followed by ...♗e6. But having played ...g6, taking with the g-pawn is certainly more logical for a human.
11.d4 h4 12.dxc5 ♗xc5+ 13.♗e3 ♗e7 14.h3

Seirawan noted that the h-pawn became a perpetual weakness, and he

would soon be tied up on both flanks as a result.
14...b6 15.♕e2 ♘b8 16.♖fd1 ♗a6 17.♕e1 ♘d7 18.b4 ♘f8 19. a4 ♗c4 20.♘cd4 ♕d7

With the intention to justify ...♕d7 by sacrificing the exchange.
21.b5 ♘g6
Yasser explained, 'My plan was 21... ♖c8, then 22.♘c6 ♖xc6 23.bxc6 ♕xc6 24.a5 bxa5 25.♖db1 – I've just got a very bad grovel and I'm material down to boot.'
22.♘c6 ♔f8 23.♘d2 ♗d3 24.c4 ♔g7 25.cxd5

25...exd5 If instead 25...♕xd5, the players demonstrated that White wins by 26.♘xe7 ♘xe7 27.♘f3 ♖ad8 28. ♖a3 ♕c4 29.♖c3 ♕e4 30.♕f2.
26.♘b1 ♗c4 27.♕c3 ♕e6 28. ♘d2 ♖hc8 29.♘d4 ♕d7 30.e6

Black resigned.

Nakamura, wearing sunglasses on his head, strolled into the commentary room, and was greeted by warm applause from the live audience, as he and Seirawan proceeded to briefly show their game.

'I think I just got a small advantage in the opening, and Yasser got a little bit low on time. I think he failed to come up with a good plan and basically it was easy for me to play – most of my moves were natural.'

After clinching his third U.S. Championship, Nakamura was asked why he seemed so nonchalant. No fists raised high in celebration as fans witnessed from Gata Kamsky the two years prior. He seemed bemused. 'I was *supposed* to win, I think. If I hadn't won I'd be pretty depressed. It's nice, but there are a lot of tournaments ahead.'

Game, Set ... but no Match

After clinching the title, Nakamura sent Garry Kasparov a text message on his mobile phone, to light-heartedly inquire whether he would be receiving the Best Game prize. 'It's always fun sometimes to just try and chat him up, see what he's up to these days. Of course we aren't working together anymore but you know he's still Kasparov and ever so often I will try and talk to him.'

By the time of the closing ceremony, just before the prize was announced, he had not received a reply. 'We'll see (laughs) if he chooses to punish me even further for that' – a reference to Nakamura's decision to cut short their training relationship, for which he assumes Kasparov might hold a grudge.

Decisions over which events to play was one point of contention between them. By year's end Nakamura felt he had been playing too much. For 2012, he thinks he's found a better balance.

'Taking a long break after Wijk aan Zee is pretty bad, but I have three tournaments this summer, which I feel is the right amount. Nothing is back-to-back quite like it was last year, so I'm feeling quite confident. Hopefully I can play well in Moscow and Biel, but for me the main tournament is definitely the Olympiad (...) I feel like this is one of the last opportunities that I'm going to have during my career to possibly win a team gold medal, and having the chance to do that I think tops almost everything else you can achieve besides becoming World Champion.'

Nakamura's concerned that none of the younger players, like Hess and Robson, will pursue chess to the 2700 level, to fill Kamsky's place on the team. Gata continues to insist that he will retire from chess once he turns forty. 'I made a decision a long time ago, and I'm going to stick by it. Because the way I see it right now, the way I play chess, is like I see less and less during the [game], and that's not a good trend.'

U.S. Champion and 5th in the world rankings. Hikaru Nakamura celebrates with his parents

Gelfand's performance in the cycle and the match impressed him, but he still sees the next World Cup as his very last chance to pursue the world title. He is not one of the participants in the next Candidates' tournament. 'I'm actually happy that I'm out of the cycle', he remarked at the closing ceremony, noting that it has been nearly five years since he could say that. 'I feel like I need rest because I have no life.'

Kamsky is more upbeat about the Americans' prospects in Istanbul. 'Our team is going to be one unit, a phalanx, so to speak, and we're going to try our best, and I have a good feeling about

this Olympiad.' But, as for the title of U.S. Champion, he says, 'The strongest this year won, so, I'm content.'

After Viswanathan Anand's slip in the ratings following the match, Nakamura has moved to number 5 in the world on live ratings, at 2782.6 – his personal best. A shot at the World Championship remains his goal, but following FIDE's current trajectory, that possibility is at least three or four years away.

He still needs a team, but at least that gives him time to strengthen his backhand, learn how to volley, and fine tune his serve.

St Louis 2012				1	2	3	4	5	6	7	8	9	10	11	12		cat. XVI
																	TPR
1 Hikaru Nakamura	IGM	USA	2775	*	1	½	½	½	½	1	1	1	½	1	1	8½	2831
2 Gata Kamsky	IGM	USA	2741	0	*	1	½	1	1	½	½	0	1	1	1	7½	2757
3 Alexander Onischuk	IGM	USA	2660	½	0	*	½	½	½	½	1	1	½	1	½	6½	2696
4 Yuri Shulman	IGM	USA	2571	½	½	½	*	½	½	½	½	½	½	½	1	6	2675
5 Aleksandr Lenderman	IGM	USA	2587	½	0	½	½	*	½	1	½	½	1	½	½	6	2674
6 Varuzhan Akobian	IGM	USA	2625	½	0	½	½	½	*	0	1	1	1	0	1	6	2670
7 Ray Robson	IGM	USA	2614	0	½	½	½	0	1	*	1	½	1	½	0	5½	2635
8 Robert Hess	IGM	USA	2635	0	½	0	½	½	0	0	*	1	½	1	1	5	2597
9 Gregory Kaidanov	IGM	USA	2594	0	1	0	½	½	0	½	0	*	0	1	½	4	2535
10 Alejandro Ramirez	IGM	USA	2593	½	0	½	½	0	0	0	½	1	*	1	0	4	2535
11 Alexander Stripunsky	IGM	USA	2562	0	0	0	½	½	1	½	0	0	0	*	1	3½	2507
12 Yasser Seirawan	IGM	USA	2643	0	0	½	0	½	0	1	0	½	1	0	*	3½	2499

Irina's Journey

Running concurrently with the U.S. Championship, the Women's Championship was similarly a two horse race. IMs Irina Krush and Anna Zatonskih have, between them, won the past seven women's titles, across a variety of formats. Sometimes the title has gone to the highest scoring woman in the main U.S. Championship, other times a separate tournament has been held.

In 2011, a qualifying Swiss tournament led to four-player knockout matches, which pit Krush (5½/7) and Zatonskih (4/7) against each other in the semi-finals. After trading wins Zatonskih won an Armageddon game, and advanced to eventually win her fourth title.

This year, in a round-robin format, the pair were two steps ahead of the field for most of the Championship, and finished tied on 7/9. A rapid play-off decided the title and Krush won both games.

'Playoffs were always a very difficult and stressful thing for me', Krush confessed later. 'I could pay *anything* to avoid a playoff.'

She was in good shape psychologically, which was a significant factor, although Krush says she played on the lower end of her abilities overall. By contrast, winning in 2010 with 8/9 against similar opposition was a closer expression of what she is capable of. 'It's funny in a way – it's only like a point difference, right? It seems like it's not a lot,' she said, adding, 'that one point is a huge difference in terms of how convincingly and powerfully you're playing.'

Irina says she tends to adapt to the needs of the tournament, pushing herself to keep pace with a rival. That was especially true in 2010, but also this year, when she won her last game with black against third-ranked WGM Camilla Baginskaite to reach the playoff.

Another factor in her psychological stability was the presence of her coach

2012 U.S. Women's Champion Irina Krush: 'September 17th – it was a day that changed my life.'

MACAULEY PETERSON

GM Georgi Kacheishvili, with whom she first studied as a teenager in 1999, until he returned to his native Georgia. Ten years later, after he immigrated to New York on a more permanent basis, they reunited and have been working together ever since.

Krush has learned about more than just chess from Kacheishvili. Long arguments with Georgi, a devout Christian, over religion and God prompted a curiosity about Christianity, that culminated in a spiritual

conversion of sorts. Although coming from a Jewish family, Irina was not raised in a religious tradition. 'All of religion was basically outside of the sphere of my interest, up until that point.'

'It's not anything that I felt was missing, or that I was looking for. I didn't have any need for this. There was no crisis in my life, there was no unhappiness in my life', she explains. Rather, a persistent exposure to Kacheishvili's worldview (although she stresses he is not evangelical about his beliefs) gradually won her over. While initially setting out to argue *against* her teacher, 'In the end, the mountain didn't move, you know? I moved towards the mountain.'

Shortly after another St. Louis event, the Kings versus Queens match held last September, she was invited by fellow U.S. Championship competitor Alex Lenderman, who is also a student of Kacheishvili, to attend a Russian Orthodox church in Bayonne, New Jersey, for Saturday evening services.

'September 17th – it was a day that changed my life', she recalls with a smile. She had never been to a church service before, in fact she says, 'I never admired the architecture of churches, I didn't like to go into them, it was sort of scary for me.' And yet, she describes a sense of awe and a divine presence that was gratifying. She began going more regularly, and was baptized on December 24th, her twenty-eighth birthday.

En route to the Women's title, Krush effected a crucial escape over former Champion Rusudan Goletiani.

NOTES BY
Irina Krush

OI 14.4 – A43
Irina Krush
Rusudan Goletiani
St. Louis 2012 (6)

This game could have completely changed the tournament standings. I was a half point ahead of Anna, and a point ahead of Rusa, but I was very close to dropping down to a tie for second-third place with a loss. It was by far the most exciting game I played in Saint Louis, one that etches itself in your memory.
1.d4 ♘f6 2.♘f3 c5 3.d5 d6 4. ♘c3 e5 5.e4 ♗e7 6.h3 h5 7.g3 ♘bd7 8.♗e2 ♘f8 9.♔f1 ♘g6 10. h4 ♘g4 11.♘g5 ♘f8 12.f3 ♘h6

13.♗e3 a6 14.a4 f6 15.♘h3 g5 16.♕d2 ♘f7 17.♘f2 gxh4 18. ♖xh4 f5 19.♖h1 h4 20.exf5 hxg3 21.♖xh8 ♘xh8 22.♘fe4 ♗xf5 23. ♘xg3 ♕d7 24.♔f2 ♘fg6 25.♖h1 0-0-0 26.♘xf5 ♕xf5 27.♕d3 ♕f7 28.♕e4 ♖f8

A critical moment. I liked my position, but I knew I had to do something quickly before Black could regroup with ...♘g6-f4 and ...♘h8-g6. I'd been looking for the opportunity to make b2-b4 work for a number of moves already, and this was no exception. I had around thirty minutes, but stubbornly spent more than twenty of them here, feeling that I must have something, yet unable to find it. I knew my maneuver ♗f1-h3 wasn't the solution, but I finally had to make a move.
29.♗f1 Correct was 29.b4! cxb4 30.♕c4+ ♔b8 31.♕xb4 ♘f4

ANALYSIS DIAGRAM

This was my stumbling block. The desirable 32.♗xa6 runs into 32... ♘d3+, and I didn't have the imagination to realize I could give away the bishop on e2, and the f3-square, by 32.♕b6!! (32.♖b1 is not as strong, because it gives up control of the

h4-square: 32...♗h4+ 33.♔f1 ♕d7, and there's an annoying mate threat on h3) 32...♘xe2 33.♖b1! ♕xf3+ 34.♔e1 (Black is getting mated and needs to give up her queen) 34...♕f1+ 35.♔d2 ♕xb1 36.♘xb1.
29...♘h4
Now that the f3-square is not defended, Black has this better option for the knight.
30.♗h3+ ♔b8 31.♗g4 ♕f6

The second critical moment. Black has the simple and strong plan of ...♘f7-g5, after which I have nothing to be happy about. I decided I needed to get something going on the queenside at any cost. The idea is right, but I again miss the spectacular justification for this play.
32.b4 cxb4

33.♘e2
So this pawn sacrifice starts to turn the tables on White.
I should have played 33.♕xb4!! (I just couldn't imagine that I could drop the f3-pawn and allow all sorts of discovered checks to my king, and that it would be harmless) 33...♘xf3 34.♖b1 ♘d2+ (34...♘d4+ 35.♔g2) – isn't White just losing all her pieces? –

35.♔g2, and yet it is amazing how the king is perfectly safe here: 35...♘xb1 36.♕b6! ♕f1+ 37.♔h2

ANALYSIS DIAGRAM

When I looked at this game with Gata Kamsky, he immediately pointed out my ally on h8, which so lovingly shields my king from danger on the h-file. How I would have loved to put all this on the board, and yet how totally out of my reach it is ☺.

33...a5 34.c3 ♕g6 35.♕c4

I thought that trading queens might be the correct 'bail out' choice (bail out into a still worse position for White), but I decided to take my chances with the queens on the board.

35...♘xf3!

In my time-trouble, I underestimated this move. I only checked that ...♘xf3 followed by ...e4 doesn't work, and completely missed that Black can play ...♕f5.

I was more concerned with 35...bxc3, since I can't recapture the pawn, but I found some comfort in the move 36. ♗b6, which apparently wins for White!

36.♗xf3 ♕f5

If 36...e4 then 37.♘f4.

37.♘g1

Irina Krush: 'Playoffs were always a very difficult and stressful thing for me. I could pay *anything* to avoid a playoff.'

37...♘g6

A nice move. During the game, in my oblivion, I actually felt some relief here, because I have a move to do something. But as it turns out, it's not easy to use this move well. The computer says that the best defense is 38.♔g3, which, needless to say, with my one minute on the clock, I didn't consider.

On 37...e4 I was counting on 38.♕d4, but it looks like it's not quite enough:

ANALYSIS DIAGRAM

38...♘g6! 39.♕a7+ ♔c8 40.♕a8+

♔c7 41.♕xa5+ ♔d7 42.♕xb4 (42.♕b5+ ♔c8) 42...♔c8, White is running out of checks and Black will recapture on f3 soon. However, in time-pressure it's not so easy to calculate that ♕d4 doesn't lead anywhere, so Rusa's choice looks more logical.

38.♔e1 ♕b1+ 39.♗d1

This was my 'human' defense. It loses, but fortunately not in a super obvious way, and certainly not obvious with our clock situation.

39...♖c8

A natural and strong move, that doesn't let out the win.

Comp suggests 39...b3, with the point 40.♕xb3 ♕d3! 41.♗f2 ♗h4!, crushing for Black.

40.♕b5!?

A tough decision on move 40. I was deciding between this and the retreat ♕e2. I went for the move that at least had the possibility of creating threats of my own, and this paid off.

40...♕e4

So, we reached the time control! Finally, a chance to enjoy my... borderline losing position.

40...♗h4+ was –8, but for this –8 to be clear, you'd have to do some pretty good calculation. With some geometrical checks, Black manages to mate: 41.♔e2 ♘f4+ 42.♗xf4 ♕e4+

ANALYSIS DIAGRAM

43.♔f1 (43.♗e3 ♕g2+ 44.♔d3 ♖xc3 mate) 43...♕e1+ 44.♔g2 ♕f2+ 45.♔h3 ♕xf4, winning. I didn't appreciate the strength of 40...♗h4+ during the game at all, and what Rusa played seemed most natural and dangerous to me.

41.♕b6

I had been counting on this idea when I played 40.♕b5. Now the rook can't be taken because of 42.♕a7+ ♔c7 43. ♗b6+ ♔d7 44.♕xb7+, winning the rook on c8.

41...♖c5 42.♖h3 bxc3

This was a really difficult moment for me, and my think here used up most of the time I had been allotted after the time control, leaving me with a few minutes for the rest of the game. The lines I had been relying on were,

under closer examination, simply losing. By process of elimination I finally came upon the best defense.

43.♗c2!

I had been pinning my hopes on 43.♘e2, but 43...c2 44.♗xc5 (44. ♗xc2 also does not save White: 44...♖xc2 45.♕a7+ ♔c8 46.♕a8+ ♔d7 47.♕xb7+ ♔e8 48.♕b8+ ♔f7 49.♖h7+ ♔f6 and wins) 44... c1♕ 45.♕a7+ ♔c8 46.♕a8+ ♔d7 47.♕xb7+ ♔e8 48.♕c8+ ♔f7 49. ♖h7+ (49.♕e6+ ♔g7 and the checks end) 49...♔f6 50.♕e6+ ♔g5 and Black's king has nimbly walked himself to safety.

43...♕xc2 44.♗xc5 dxc5

One more decision to make.

45.♘e2

I was seriously considering 45.d6, with the point that after 45...♕d2+ 46.♔f1 ♕xd6 47.♕xd6+ ♗xd6 48.♖xc3 it is not so easy for Black to convert her three pawns for the exchange. Ultimately, though, I decided to take my chances in another version of being down many pawns for the exchange. It's a good thing too, because Black can improve with 45...♗h4+! 46.♖xh4 ♕c1+! 47.♔f2 ♕b2+!!, forcing the

exchange of queens and there is no one to stop the b-pawn. One of the many pretty lines that remained hidden in this game.

45...c4

This lets me off the hook too easily. Now I can execute the d6 idea in a much improved version (the knight on e2 is much more helpful to White than the pawn on c4).

I was expecting 45...♕d2+ 46.♔f1 c2 47.♕xg6 c1♕+ 48.♘xc1 ♕xc1+, and I thought I had decent chances to fight for a draw here.

46.d6 ♕d2+ 47.♔f1 ♕d1+ 48.♔f2

48...♗xd6

48...♕xd6 49.♕xd6+ ♗xd6 50.♖xc3 loses the c4-pawn immediately, so White has nothing to worry about.

49.♕d8+ ♔a7 50.♕xa5+ ♔b8 51.♕d8+ Draw.

It's fun to live on the edge, when you survive ☺.

Thanks to Rusa for her creative play! And to Rex and Jeannie and everyone at the Chess Club for once again putting on the best event of the year. ∎

St Louis 2012 women			cat. III
			TPR
1 Irina Krush	IM	2457	7	2523
2 Anna Zatonskih	IM	2510	7	2517
3 Rusudan Goletiani	IM	2333	5½	2397
4 Viktorija Ni	WIM	2228	5	2371
5 Iryna Zenyuk	WIM	2224	4½	2329
6 Sabina-Fr. Foisor	WGM	2364	4½	2313
7 Tatev Abrahamyan	WGM	2329	4½	2317
8 Alisa Melekhina	FM	2242	3½	2247
9 Camilla Baginskaite	WGM	2358	2	2094
10 Alena Kats	WFM	2137	1½	2065
Tie-break match Krush-Zatonskih won by Krush			

Charles Hertan

Forcing Moves

On the Borderline

Positions that straddle the fence between middlegame and ending are among the most devilish to play. A.Kuzmin called major piece endings 'the fourth stage of the chess game'. Although these positions often feature normal endgame themes like promotion and simplification, you won't find ♕+♖ endings in either *ChessBase* Big Database's Endgame section, or Fine's magnum opus *BCE*. Why? They are so varied, complex and tactical as to nearly defy categorization. Add a pair of minor pieces and the puzzle gets fuzzier still. The transition from middlegame to endgame is normally marked by the emerging role of king activity. But in major piece positions with even one ♕+♖ per side, an 'active' king more often than not invites a mating attack, or sufficient counterplay to compensate for a pawn or two – *unless* the king can hide behind enemy pawns, or even join the attack against its opposite number. The percentage of high level 'fourth phase' positions busted by a 'visit to the Aquarium' is embarrassing, but one master merits special mention for his virtuosity in these crazy scenarios (drum roll…) – Victor the Terrible.

For each problem, the goal is to find the quickest and clearest winning line unless otherwise noted. A 'winning line' could range from checkmate, to being a pawn up with no objective compensation for the opponent.

Level of difficulty:
1-4 stars, 1 is 'easiest' and 4 'most difficult'. The star rating refers to the difficulty of finding all the relevant variations, not just finding the right key move.

Solutions on page 105

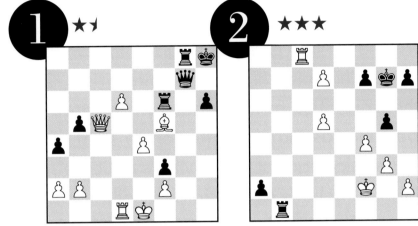

1 ★★⟋ Black to move and win

2 ★★★ Black to move and win

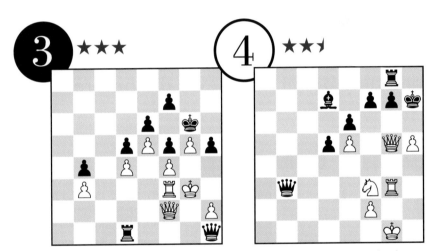

3 ★★★ Black to move and win

4 ★★⟋ White to move and win

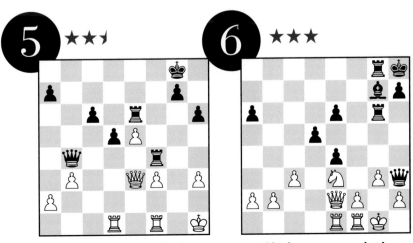

5 ★★⟋ Black to move and win

6 ★★★ Black to move and win

Hitherto available only in Spanish, Miguel Najdorf's account of the 1953 Candidates' Tournament, *15 Aspirantes al Titulo Mundial*, will reach a deserved broader readership now that it has been translated into English as *Zurich 1953: 15 Contenders for the World Chess Championship* (Russell Enterprises, 2012). While working on the translation of this under-appreciated classic, **Taylor Kingston** became fascinated by the lonely fight of American GM Samuel Reshevsky against the Soviet 'syndicate', a fight that foreshadowed Bobby Fischer's accusations of collusion at Curaçao 1962, which would finally force FIDE to change the world championship cycle.

Little did Reshevsky know what really awaited him, when on the eve of Zurich 1953 he said: 'This is going to be a tough tournament to win — probably the toughest of my career — so I'll just have to work harder and play better than I ever did before.'

Held August 30 to October 23 in the Swiss cities of Neuhausen and Zurich, the 1953 Candidates' Tournament was arguably the greatest chess tournament ever to that point, not only for its balance of quality and quantity, but also for its dramatic historical context. While AVRO 1938 and The Hague-Moscow 1948 had somewhat higher average strengths, they involved only eight and five players respectively. And while there had been many major tournaments with 15 or more players, they were almost always single round-robins, not double, and there was always a steep drop in strength toward the lower half of the table.

Zurich, however, was an all-GM field, at a time when there were only about 30 active GMs in the world. Each one was then among the world's top 20 and overall there was probably no more than a 100-point range in Elo strength. The winner would be the official challenger to World Champion Botvinnik.

The prelude, and its attendant controversy, added to the interest and drama. In the wider world, the Cold War was at one of its hotter stages, the Korean War barely over, a tense armed truce in Europe, and France losing in Vietnam. Stalin's death in March 1953 added uncertainty and turbulence to the internal Soviet situation.

While the USA and her allies were largely able to contain Soviet political and military ambitions in the 1950s, the opposite was true in chess. In that decade, Soviet dominance was at its peak. The World Champion and about half of all GMs were Soviet, they took the lion's share of major tournament prizes, and practically monopolized world title qualifying events plus Olympiads and other team matches. There was no FIDE rating system, but had there been, Soviet masters would surely have occupied seven to nine of

The top finishers in Zurich 1953: winner Smyslov together with Reshevsky, Keres and Bronstein (2nd-4th).

Sammy against the Soviets

the top ten spots, and a clear majority of the top 20.

However, in 1952 suspicions arose that this dominance was not due entirely to playing strength. The Saltsjöbaden Interzonal, which determined five qualifiers for Zurich, gave strong circumstantial evidence that the Soviets were acting as a collusive team, going easy on each other but hard against rivals. While the 1948 Interzonal and 1950 Candidates' Tournament had a reasonable number of long, hard-fought, decisive intra-Soviet games, at Saltsjöbaden 1952 every game between their contestants – Kotov, Petrosian, Taimanov, Geller and Averbakh – was drawn, all but one in only 16 to 22 moves. Save that token 49-mover, the intra-Soviet average was 19 moves, compared to their 38 against non-Soviets, and the 40-move average of the tournament as a whole.

In November 1952, the American magazine *Chess Review* commented: 'A noteworthy circumstance in the Saltsjöbaden affair was the pacific attitude of the Russian players toward one another ... Kotov, for example, who fell with fury on most of his non-Russian rivals, was content to play the shortest possible 'grandmaster draws' with his compatriots.'

And it worked! The Soviets took the top five spots, winning all the Candidate slots and shutting out the sixteen other contestants. Thus, along with Smyslov, Bronstein, Keres and Boleslavsky – seeded from the previous cycle – nine of the twelve contestants at Zurich would be Soviet players.

Reshevsky Demurs

The three others were perennial US Champion Sammy Reshevsky, former World Champion Max Euwe of Holland, and Miguel Najdorf of Argentina, who were already seeded in by FIDE. But faced with this overwhelming 9-3 Red majority and its suspect ethics, Reshevsky announced he would not play. This was reiterated later in *Chess Life* by his manager Alex Bisno: 'Could we expect Reshevsky, even if he were

world champion, to defeat, in a single tournament, 9 Russian Grand Masters, all of whom would play terrifically hard against him and easily against each other. From every standpoint, the arrangement is unfair and inequitable, and I shall not blame Reshevsky at all if he refuses to compete in the Candidates' Tournament.'

Chess Review used even stronger terms in an editorial titled 'Syndicate Chess' in March 1953: 'We are worried by this tournament. We want it to be won by the best player ... We are ready to salute him – no matter who he is; no matter what his nation – *provided that he wins it fairly*. The Russians have a different attitude. They do not care who wins – or even how he wins – *just so long as he's a Russian!* But each Russian player is an agent of his state ... They play as a team: a syndicate ... *We are casting no aspersions.* In the Soviet ideology, the state is paramount ... Rather, we are paying them a compliment. We are saying that Soviet chessplayers are very good Soviet citizens ... Our sense of ethics is different. A tournament which is rigged fills the Western chess-lover with nausea *[emphasis in original].*

On the other hand, then-IM Larry Evans, who in later years would be a confirmed Commie-basher, expressed skepticism in the *Chess Life* of May 20, 1953: 'I disagree with the editorial policies of certain American chess journals which intimate collusion amongst the Russians, with little proof except what might be termed paranoiac doubts. Reshevsky, should he play, will be playing them **one at a time**, with adequate rest days in between. It is true that the Soviets will have superior analysis on their adjourned games due to their almost grandmaster seconds. It is also true, and only natural, that they will be out gunning for Sammy. But to charge

rigging of games and collusion is another matter *[emphasis in original].* Evans' doubts notwithstanding, Reshevsky remained obdurate. This and other pressures prompted FIDE around April 1953 to expand the Candidates' Tournament roster. Added were Gligoric of Yugoslavia, Szabo of Hungary, and Stahlberg of Sweden. These three had actually tied with Averbakh for 5th place at the Interzonal, and the fact that the Russian had been awarded the last slot by the tiniest tie-break margin had only exacerbated the resentment in western circles. FIDE's action was viewed, except perhaps in Moscow, as correcting an injustice.

> 'The Russians have a different attitude. They do not care who wins – or even how he wins – just so long as he's a Russian!'

Still, Reshevsky demurred, rather than play with a somewhat bigger but still stacked deck. Before and after the Interzonal he tried to bypass the Soviets' numerical advantage, publicly challenging Botvinnik, and 1951 USSR Champion Keres, to one-on-one non-title matches. These offers were simply ignored by Soviet authorities. They also backed out of a USSR-USA team match, planned for June 1953 in New York, that would have pitted Reshevsky and Botvinnik.

About all Reshevsky could do was reinforce his status as unofficial 'Champion of the Western World,' which he did by winning matches with Najdorf (+8 –4 =6) and Gligoric (+2 –1 =7) in 1952, and again with Najdorf (+6 –5 =7) in mid-1953. With Euwe in decline and Reuben Fine retired (and young Bobby Fischer an unknown novice), Reshevsky was unquestionably the best player in the world outside the USSR, which made his absence from Zurich all the more frustrating to chess fans.

However, frustration turned to elation when, *mirabile dictu*, in late August 1953, less than a week before the opening ceremony, Reshevsky announced he would play! Organizers had to scramble to rework the schedule and program, but were glad to do so. I have been unable to find out exactly why or when he changed his mind. Perhaps the 11th-hour acceptance was a ploy like the mind-games and brinksmanship by Fischer in 1972, to throw his rivals off-balance psychologically.

Mind-games or not, Reshevsky would need every edge he could get. Not only did the Soviets field nine great GMs, but also an army of seconds – Flohr, Lilienthal, Bondarevsky, Simagin, Tolush et al – scarcely inferior to the contestants themselves. The seconds' most important tasks would be adjourned game analysis (in those days, unfinished games were typically suspended after five hours and resumed at a later date), and opening research. The non-Soviets had seconds too: GM Petar Trifunovic for Gligoric, soon-to-be-IM Julio Bolbochan for Najdorf, future IM Carel van den Berg for Euwe, two-time Swedish Champion Kristian Sköld for Stahlberg, and IM Tibor Florian for Szabo.

But Reshevsky had ... Mrs. Reshevsky! Rather than a strong American master such as Evans or Fine, he brought his wife and two children. While their emotional support was probably considerable, their usefulness for chess analysis was nil.

This being like bringing a penknife to a gun fight, one wonders why. Reshevsky himself explained, in the 12/1953 *Chess Review*: 'You know how these things go in the United States. Those who would like to come and who could help – they can't afford it. Whatever I do in this tournament, I've got to do it myself.' As we will see, lack of a second would prove crucial.

Lucky and Unlucky Breaks
While both Smyslov and Reshevsky played very well at Zurich, looking closely at their games, I was surprised at the number of close calls and lucky (or unlucky) breaks both experienced. Had these gone differently, the final standings could have changed greatly.

'But Reshevsky had ... Mrs. Reshevsky! Rather than a strong American master such as Evans or Fine, he brought his wife and two children.'

For example, Euwe-Smyslov in Round 3. The Dutch GM had started like the champ he used to be, beating Kotov and Geller, then attacking Smyslov's Grünfeld so aggressively that the Russian lost his way and fell into a critical situation at move 28:

Euwe-Smyslov
position after 27...fxe5

With 28.♕d6! Euwe could have forced Black to return the exchange, giving White a probably winning endgame, viz. 28...♕a6+ 29.♕xa6 ♘xa6 30.♘xb8 ♖xb8 31.♖e1, or 28...♖xd7 29.♕xd7 ♕c5 30.♔g1 ♖f8 31.♕d2. Smyslov might even have fallen into 28...♖b6? 29.♕e7 ♘c6?? 30.♕f6+ ♔g8 31.♗h3 and Black is crushed. As it was, Euwe played **28.♕d2?.** The ensuing time scramble created a maddeningly murky position which, upon post-adjournment resumption, seemed to portend only endless checks and wood-shifting. But finally, a fatigued Euwe blundered.

position after 57...♔h7

With 58.♖d5! White still had good chances to hold, but Euwe played **58. ♖b6??** and after **58...♕c7!**, threatening 59...♘g4, he resigned.

Smyslov got even luckier in Round 11. Confused by an ingenious Bronstein novelty

Smyslov-Bronstein
postion after 13...♘xg4

he played **14.e4??** (better 14.♘f3), overlooking that 14...♗a3! wins, viz. 15.♕xg4 ♗xb2 16.♘a3 ♗xa3 and

Black is two pawns up, or 15.♗xa3 ♕xh4 and the mate threats cost major material. However, as Bronstein explained in his own book on the tournament, he could not calculate the latter variation fully, missing that after 16.♖e1 ♕xf2+ 17.♔h1 ♕h4+ 18.♔g1 ♘de5! 19.♗xf8 ♖xf8 White, though temporarily a rook up, is utterly crushed. And so he played **14...♘xf2?!** and the game was eventually drawn. A very lucky escape against probably the best tactician in the world, who of all the Soviet players probably was the least comfortable with the 'syndicate' philosophy.

Next round, Smyslov got a gift point when a sleep-deprived Gligoric blundered a pawn in a virtually even position. And in Round 17, Szabo had Smyslov on the ropes, but the game was eventually drawn.

On the other hand, Smyslov missed a win in Round 15:

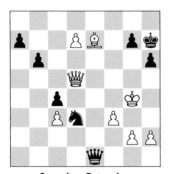

Smyslov-Petrosian
position after 46.d7

Here Petrosian could have maintained equality with 46...♘e5+ 47.♕xe5 ♕xe5 48.d8♕ ♕e6+ 49.♔g3 ♕e5+

50.♔f2 ♕xc3 etc. Instead he played a seductive move found in home analysis, the study-like **46...♕e5** and Smyslov, mesmerized by its apparent beauty and seemingly unanswerable threats of 47...♕xd5 or mate by 47...♘f2+ or 47...♕f4+, played **47.♕xd3+? cxd3 48.d8♕** and then agreed to a draw. At the time players, seconds and spectators all unanimously praised this 'brilliant coup,' and Najdorf gave it '!!' in his notes. Months later a Dutch amateur showed that it actually deserved '??' because 47.♕d6! wins in all variations.

Smyslov got 3½ points from these five games. It could have been four, which would have made no difference. On the other hand, it could have been only one, in which case, *ceteris paribus*, he would have ended up 4th, with Bronstein 1st, and Reshevsky and Keres shared 2nd-3rd.

Reshevsky was perhaps even luckier. Against Keres in Round 11 he misplayed the black side of a Nimzo-Indian and after just 14 moves was in critical danger:

Keres-Reshevsky
position after 14...♕c7

Here 15.exf6 was best, giving White a significant if not winning advantage. But Keres played the second-best **15.♗xf6 gxf6** and then thought for an hour before finally continuing **16.♕g4+ ♔h8 17.♕f3?** (better 17.exf6), whereupon with **17...♘d7!** Reshevsky was out of trouble and the game eventually drawn. Instead, later analysis concluded that 16.f4! could have won for White.

Yet this was nothing compared to Szabo-Reshevsky in Round 19. Sammy got into time-trouble even worse and sooner than usual, and by move 20 had only *one minute* left for his next 21 moves! Thus, after 20.♘f6+

Szabo-Reshevsky
position after 20.♘f6+

he played the egregious **20...♗xf6??** Yet miraculously Szabo, who still had *30 minutes* on his clock, somehow missed the screamingly obvious 21.♕xg6+ with mate next, playing instead **21.♗xf6?** Even so, he got a second chance after **21...♗xd5 22.cxd5 ♕d6 23.♕c3 ♕xd5 24.♖fd1 ♕f5 25.e4?** when instead of 25...♕xe4 with equality, Reshevsky

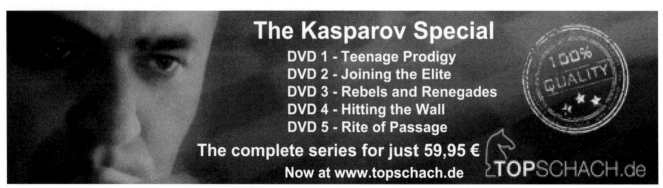

played **25...♕e6?**, then compounded the error with **26.♗g7 b6??**

Now, with 27.♗h6! f6 28.♕g3, threatening both 29.♕xg6+ and 29.♕xb8, Szabo again could have forced resignation, but amazingly he played **27. ♗xf8?** and after **27...♔xf8** despite his still better position, his nerves were so shattered that he offered a draw, which Reshevsky gladly accepted.

Reshevsky also benefited when Averbakh blundered in an even position. So in those three games Reshevsky netted two points, when he might well have had only a half. *Ceteris paribus*, that would have consigned him way down to shared 5th-7th with Najdorf and Geller, behind Smyslov, Keres, Bronstein, and Petrosian.

If fortune favoured Reshevsky in those games, it went against him with Taimanov in Round 15. Again in time pressure, Reshevsky still managed to outplay the Russian in the middlegame, but failed to convert his advantage and let him escape with a draw.

Far more glaring, though, and surely more galling, was Reshevsky's failure with Geller in Round 24, going into which Reshevsky and Smyslov were tied for 1st, ½ point ahead of Keres and Bronstein. The game was adjourned in a position Najdorf called 'absolutely winning for White'.

Reshevsky-Geller
position after 41.♔h2

Objectively true, but one factor was overwhelmingly in Black's favour: Reshevsky had no second, but Geller, because his opponent was the Soviets'

only real rival, could call on their entire team! Thus Reshevsky could afford few mistakes. But mistakes there were. Play continued **41...♖e1 42.f4 ♖e3 43.♖g4 ♔h7 44.♖g3 ♖e2 45.h4 ♖e4 46.♖f3 f6 47.exf6 gxf6**

Here, as Najdorf and Euwe point out, with 48.g4! White could have started clinching the win, but Reshevsky began to go astray with **48.♔g3?!**, blocking his pawn. **48...♔g6 49. ♖a3** Beginning a faulty plan. Najdorf recommends 49.f5+ ♔h5 50.♖f4 ♖e3+ 51.♔h2 followed by g2-g3 and ♔h2-h3. **49...f5 50.♖a6+?** Better 50.♔f3 and if 50...♔h5 51.g4+! wins. **50...♔h5 51.♖f6?** Unlikely as it might seem, this move, by which White gets Black's last pawn, makes it impossible to win. Najdorf recommends 51.♖a8, a move later endorsed by Kasparov. **51...♖e3+ 52.♔f2 ♖a3 53.g3?** Why did Reshevsky not play 53.♖xf5+ ♔xh4, giving himself two connected passed pawns and a seeming easy win? Perhaps because he realized that the resulting position:

ANALYSIS DIAGRAM

is actually a theoretical draw! For example 54.g3+ ♖xg3 55.♖h5+ ♔xh5

56.♔xg3 ♔g6, or 54.♖g5 ♖a2+ 55.♔g1 (if 55.♔e3 ♖e2+) 55...♖a1+ 56.♔h2 ♖h1+! 57.♔xh1 stalemate, or 54.♖f8 ♔g4! 55.f5 ♔g5 56.f6 ♔g6 and White can get nowhere.

Still 53.♖xf5+ was the best try, because the text let Black clinch the draw immediately with **53...♖f3+!!**

This startling shot had been foreseen by the Russian team in their adjournment analysis. Now 54.♔xf3 is stalemate. Reshevsky sought another way, but ultimately in vain. **54.♔e2 ♖xg3 55.♖xf5+ ♔xh4 56.♔f2 ♖a3 57. ♖g5 ♖b3 58.♖g1 ♔h5 59.♔e2 ♖a3 60.f5 ♖a5** ½-½

The Syndicate Steps In
Reshevsky could not have known (though he may have suspected) that around this time the Soviet 'syndicate' really started pulling strings to hinder him and help Smyslov. For this our main source is none other than Bronstein. Though he said nothing at the time, nearly fifty years later he would reveal, first in a 2001 article in the Russian magazine *64*, and later in his posthumously published memoir *Secret Notes* (2007 Edition Olms), the machinations behind the scenes. His revelations were also examined in a 2002 ChessCafe.com article by GM Andy Soltis, *Treachery in Zurich*.

Standings at the halfway point of the tournament, after 15 rounds, were as follows:
1. Smyslov 9½-4½; 2-3. Reshevsky, Bronstein 8½-5½; 4. Najdorf 8-6; 5-7. Boleslavsky, Euwe, Petrosian 7½-6½; 8-9. Keres, Taimanov 7-7; 10. Kotov 6½-7½; 11-14. Averbakh, Geller,

Gligoric, Szabo 6-8; 15. Stahlberg 3½-10½.

Bronstein says about this time the team doctor, Vladimir Ridin, reported to Dmitri Postnikov, chief of the Soviet group, that 'Keres and Bronstein were in a normal condition whereas Smyslov had weakened and might not last.' This diagnosis was borne out by Kotov-Smyslov in Round 21:

Those were the days! Vasily Smyslov and Samuel Reshevsky share memories at a veterans' tournament in Moscow in 1991.

position after 19.♖fd1

Here, standing no worse than even, Smyslov played **19...♘d5?!** apparently believing he would win White's pinned knight at c3. Kotov made the forced reply **20.♖xd5** whereupon Smyslov played **20...♗xc3??** and Kotov, with what must have been the sharpest of mixed feelings, played **21.♖xd7! ♖xd7 22.♗xc3** giving him two pieces for the rook and a won game (1-0, 40).

Mixed feelings because Kotov, who had started with only two points in eight games, was surely delighted to beat the hitherto undefeated leader, but he was also the most zealous of Communists, the reddest of Reds, and it must have pained him to hurt the cause of Socialist Culture.

As a result, Smyslov slipped into a tie with Reshevsky, who started the second half strongly with five points in seven games. More importantly, it convinced the Soviet 'triumvirate' – Postnikov (deputy chairman of the Sports Committee), KGB officer Moshintsev, and GM Igor Bondarevsky – that more than chess moves were required to stop the American.

Their cause was helped in Round 23, when Kotov atoned for beating Smyslov by defeating Reshevsky. The American GM again mishandled an adjourned ending, though this time he erred trying to win an even game, rather than botching a win.

In the next round, the triumvirate took a direct hand. They had already intervened, though not unethically, by ordering Bronstein to beat Reshevsky in Round 13, which he did. Now, however, they 'summoned Keres to the shore of the Zurich lake and over the course of three hours tried to persuade him to make a quick draw with white against Smyslov.'

Keres must have greatly resented this. Not only did it bring back memories of 1948, when he had been subjected to pressure on Botvinnik's behalf, but also in recent rounds he had been playing very well, scoring +4 –0 =4 to rise into serious contention, only ½ point behind Smyslov. Meekly foregoing a chance to overtake him went strongly against his grain. And with the normally chilling Soviet political climate thawing slightly, Keres seems to have felt bold enough to resist.

However, says Bronstein, Keres arrived to the game 'all flushed and agitated ... not in a fit state to play.' Overreaching, he launched an unsound attack, which Smyslov deftly refuted:

Keres-Smyslov
position after 15...♘c6

16.♘e5? Better 16.c5 with equality. **16...♘xe5 17.♖xe5 ♗f6 18.♖h5?** Objectively better was 18.♖e2, though Black would still stand better. **18...g6 19.♖ch3**

19...dxc4! Not 19...gxh5? 20.♕xh5 ♖e8 21.a4! (to allow ♗a3) and wins. **20.♖xh7 c3! 21.♕c1 ♕xd4!** Not 21...cxb2?? 22.♕h6 ♕xd4 23. ♖h8+ ♗xh8 24.♕h7 mate. **22.♕h6 ♖fd8 23.♗c1 ♗g7 24.♕g5 ♕f6**

25.♕g4 c2 26.♗e2 ♖d4 27.f4 ♖d1+ 28.♗xd1 ♕d4+ 0-1

Reshevsky Faces Smyslov

Despite Smyslov's windfall, Reshevsky could still keep pace by winning his adjourned game with Geller. That would not resume, however, until after Round 25, when Smyslov and Reshevsky would meet for the second time.

When they first played, in Round 10, Reshevsky was leading the field, ½ point ahead of Smyslov. Despite having White he made no great effort to win, and a calm 19-move draw resulted. Now, however, he could little afford complacency. Assuming he did beat Geller, he would still technically be tied for first, but in fact Smyslov had a game in hand, because his bye had already come, while Reshevsky's would be in Round 27. Thus it behoved Reshevsky to try for a win.

All the more surprising, then, that he chose a seldom-used and unpromising opening, and within the first 20 moves surrendered the bishop pair, incurred a permanent positional weakness, and reduced himself to passive defence with little hope beyond a draw with best play.

Smyslov-Reshevsky
position after 22.♕c3

Here was probably Reshevsky's last chance for counterplay, by 22...f5, which his previous move 21...♘f6-h5 seemed to prepare. Yet instead he inexplicably indulged in pointless waiting moves, shuffling his knight, king and queen back and forth, allowing Smyslov, who at this point had about an hour more on his clock, to work out a breakthrough plan at leisure.

22...♘f6 23.e4 ♘h5 24.♕e3 ♘f6 25.♗h3 ♘h7 26.♖e2 ♘f6 27.♖f1 ♘h5 'The knight continues its dance.' (Najdorf) **28.♗g2 ♕e7 29.♗c1 ♕c7 30.♖d1 ♔h7 31.♕f2 ♘f6 32.♗e3 ♘h5 33.♖c2**

Black's position is exactly as at move 22, except the king is on h7, not g8. Now with White threatening a queenside break by a2-a3 and b3-b4, Reshevsky finally does what he should have done at move 22, but here it has a fatal flaw. **33...f5? 34.exf5 gxf5 35.g4!**

35...♘f4 Black must accept the loss of a pawn, since if 35...fxg4?? 36.♕h4 and the pinned knight is lost. Now it is only a matter of time and technique, and Smyslov had plenty of both. **36. ♗xf4 exf4 37.♕h4+ ♔g8 38.gxf5 d5 39.cxd5** and Reshevsky resigned at move 56.

'Did you really think we came here to play chess?'

This loss, and his failure with Geller, left Reshevsky 1½ points back, and with only four games left to Smyslov's five, his chances of overtaking the Russian were slim. The Soviet triumvirate,

however, with its goal now clearly in sight, was not content to leave anything to chance. Before Round 25, they summoned Bronstein. In *Secret Notes* he reports the conversation: 'Now,' said Postnikov, lighting up another cigarette ... 'After [this round] you have Smyslov. Remember that before his game with Reshevsky he must not be agitated! He must know that you will make a quick draw with him.' – 'But I have White!' – 'What's the difference? We cannot risk an American winning the tournament.' – 'But I too can win ...' – 'A draw and a quick one! ... We have just received a coded telegram from [Sports Committee Chairman Nikolai] Romanov: "Play between the Soviet participants is to cease." Do you understand?' I was stupefied by such falsehood. My look did not appeal to Moshintsev, and he decided to intensify the pressure by blurting out 'What, did you really think we came here to play chess?' Bronstein considered resisting, but his main political ally, Boris Vainstein (for Genna Sosonko's portrait of Vainstein see New In Chess 2011/6), was incommunicado back in Russia, and with Vainstein's post-Stalin status uncertain, Bronstein did not have the clout to gainsay Postnikov and Moshintsev. So, reluctantly, he agreed to the charade with Smyslov, playing a thoroughly tepid Exchange Ruy Lopez. He records that as he played 4.♗xc6 Reshevsky walked past. 'On seeing my move, he stopped and made an expressive "Hmm ..." I can still hear that sound, because the shame has not gone away.'

And with this 'Hmm' Reshevsky seems to have accepted the futility of further effort, drawing with Keres even more quickly. Then, what slight chance Reshevsky still had vanished in Round 28, when he threw away a probable win against Bronstein. This made his score for Rounds 23-28 +0 –3 =2, a bleak streak just when he needed to be at his best.

Meanwhile Smyslov coasted home with five draws averaging less than 18 moves. Reshevsky salvaged some pride by beating Gligoric in Round 29 and finishing tied for 2nd-4th with Bronstein and Keres, two points behind.

Could Reshevsky Have Won?

Was it within the realm of reasonable possibility that, had these crucial games gone differently, had the breaks broken the other way, Reshevsky could have won? It depends very much on one's definition of 'reasonable.'

In the most unfavourable scenario, Reshevsky could have fared much worse. Smyslov could have beaten Petrosian instead of drawing in Round 15, while Reshevsky could have lost to Keres in Round 11, and certainly to Szabo in Round 19, instead of drawing. That adds ½ point to Smyslov's score and deducts one from Reshevsky, which, *ceteris paribus*, would have relegated Sammy to 4th place, 3½ points back, with Smyslov, Keres and Bronstein sole 1st, 2nd and 3rd respectively. And failing to beat Averbakh in Round 18 would have put him even further down.

In the best-case scenario, tweaking every might-have-been to go against Smyslov or for Reshevsky, we get these changes:

Smyslov: Euwe, rd. 3: loss instead of win; Bronstein, rd. 11: loss instead of draw; Gligoric, rd. 12: draw instead of win; Szabo, rd. 17: loss instead of draw; Keres, rd. 24: draw instead of win.

Reshevsky: Taimanov, rd. 15: win instead of draw; Kotov, rd. 23: draw instead of loss; Geller, rd. 24: win instead of draw; Bronstein, rd. 28: win instead of loss.

This subtracts three points from Smyslov and ½ point from Bronstein, and gives 2½ points to Reshevsky and ½ to Keres. Other things being equal, that would make the top final standings: 1. Reshevsky 18½, 2. Keres 16½, 3. Bronstein 15½, 4. Smyslov 15. A Reshevsky rout!

But in this alternate universe, we are giving Reshevsky the benefit of *every* doubt. Making it especially improbable is that his real results were not just random flukes; they derived in part from fundamental, systemic problems: his lack of a second, his sub-par opening knowledge, and his habitual time mismanagement. Changing the first would have required significantly more funding at a time when American sponsors made Scrooge look generous. And changing the latter two would have required Reshevsky to stop being Reshevsky!

But let us indulge in fantasy. Would the 'other things' then have stayed equal? I doubt it. In the best-case scenario, after 24 rounds Reshevsky, with

> 'Chess Review pointed out "flagrant coaching from the sidelines" and "autograph seekers" passing messages to players from seconds'

15½ points, would have led, 1½ points ahead of Bronstein and two ahead of Keres, with no other Soviet player in realistic contention. It is doubtful that the triumvirate would have let things go this far this late. They would almost certainly have acted earlier.

The strategy of pre-arranged quick draws, as seen at the Interzonal (and later at Curaçao 1962) would not have worked. Someone would have to be chosen – by the players themselves, or by the triumvirate – as 'designated winner' to whom the other Soviet players would lose.

Some earlier games would probably have been rigged, with low-standing Soviets losing to contenders, e.g. Kotov to Keres (Round 22), and Boleslavsky and Kotov to Bronstein (Rounds 23 and 24). Smyslov might even have been ordered to lose to Keres in Round 24! And surely Geller would have been ordered to lose to Bronstein in Round 25, a reversal of what actually happened. (In fact, Bronstein was assured by the triumvirate that Geller had agreed to lose, but when Bronstein objected to this and other fixing, Bondarevsky secretly instructed Geller to win, to punish Bronstein for his 'greed.')

Also Reshevsky could expect no more easy games. His remaining Soviet opponents would play all out; he would have had no short draws with Keres and Taimanov as actually did occur. They might well try to extend his games to adjournment, where the Soviet analytical team would have the edge. They might even cheat overtly by passing suggested moves to his opponents during play. (*Chess Review* pointed out 'flagrant coaching from the sidelines' and 'autograph seekers' passing messages to players from seconds.)

Still, while simple in theory, this is tricky in practice. The fixed games would have to look real. They couldn't just play Scholar's Mate or leave pieces *en prise*. It's much easier to improvise colourless draws than to devise plausible GM-quality decisive games.

Furthermore, deciding victor vs. sacrificial lambs would have been no easy matter. Keres and Bronstein had bristled at official interference; Smyslov might well also if it was not on his behalf.

I have no idea how this hypothetical crisis would have turned out, but as an American, I find it a delight to contemplate. It would have been keenly interesting to be a Russian-speaking fly on the wall while the triumvirate scrambled, telegraphing Moscow, negotiating with and/or dictating to the players, ordering seconds to compose plausible games, etc. They would also probably concoct protests and incidents, as they already had in Round 8 when after a time scramble, Kotov flew into a rage over a trivial matter and demanded Reshevsky be forfeited, on threat of total Soviet withdrawal.

The Aftermath

Interesting as such speculations are, the fact remains that no such thing happened. Smyslov played by far the steadiest chess, scoring +9 –1 =18. He became the official challenger, and next year showed he was at least Botvinnik's equal by drawing their match 12-12, which however allowed Botvinnik by rule to keep the title. Smyslov again won the next Candidates' Tournament, Amsterdam 1956, and then finally dethroned Botvinnik in 1957 by 12½-9½, only to lose the title back in a rematch in 1958. Thus Smyslov's reign lasted only one year, though he outscored Botvinnik in the three matches +18 –17 =34.

Reshevsky recovered from his bad stretch to tie for 2nd-4th, scoring +8 –4 =16. All his losses – to Smyslov, Bronstein (twice) and Kotov – were to Soviets.

Since 2nd place carried with it a bid to the next Candidates' Tournament, a tie-break playoff was to be held. When Keres and Bronstein decided not to join it, the bid defaulted to Reshevsky. According to Bronstein, he and Keres skipped the playoff simply because the Interzonal gave them an extra chance to travel abroad, to Göteborg, Sweden, where they easily qualified. However, lacking funds and/or a desire to face yet another Soviet-dominated field, Reshevsky declined. Additionally Larry Evans declined a place in the 1955 Interzonal and the U.S. fielded no Olympiad team, making 1955-56 bleak years for American chess. Reshevsky would never again be a serious title contender.

He could at least take satisfaction from the USA-USSR team matches of 1954 and 1955, where he held Smyslov even, +0 –0 =4, and edged Botvinnik +1 –0 =3, indicating what he might have done had the Soviets accepted his direct challenges.

Does It Matter?

When Soviet cheating is discussed – as with Zurich here, or The Hague-Moscow 1948, Saltsjöbaden 1952, or Curaçao 1962 – two issues are often conflated: One, did it matter? And two, was it wrong? Some Soviet apologists, *e.g.* Averbakh, have argued that Fischer's complaints about Curaçao can be dismissed because it made no difference, since Fischer was never really in contention.

I find this argument absurd, like saying we should ignore murder because everyone dies anyway. Sure, Smyslov was a truly great player and might have well still won, or Reshevsky failed, had everything been completely above board. And while it might be considered unsporting for the Soviet brain

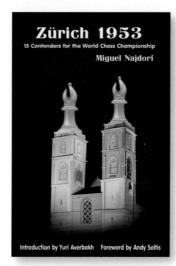

Miguel Najdorf
Zürich 1953 – 15 Contenders for the World Chess Championship
Russell Enterprises 2012

trust to gang up on Reshevsky in terms of opening preparation and adjournment analysis, it was not unethical or illegal by prevailing FIDE rules and customs.

But that hardly excuses the collusion, the fixing of games, and outside assistance during actual play. When comparable cheating is exposed in other sports, titles and trophies are taken away, games are retroactively forfeited, players are suspended or even banned. Chess, however, has historically been rather lax about such matters, and in the early 1950s the Soviet 'syndicate' approach was some-

thing new that FIDE was unprepared for, and slow to address.

Address it they finally did, when Fischer's charges of collusion at Curaçao 1962 were impossible to ignore. The Soviet-dominated Candidates' Tournament was changed to a series of elimination matches to which the syndicate system could not be applied. Thus Fischer did not face such a stacked deck, and eventually became World Champion, ending the Soviets' 24-year monopoly.

I like to think that Reshevsky's effort at Zurich 1953 was important groundwork that ultimately helped Fischer's cause. If Reshevsky was not the proverbial one-legged man in a kicking contest, he was at best like a lone soldier armed with pistols against a squad of machine-gunners. His valiant effort helped highlight the inequities, injustices and abuses prevalent in FIDE's system and, I believe, made the chess world more receptive to later calls for reform.

Perhaps the most eloquent tribute to Reshevsky's effort was in the 12/1953 *Chess Review*. It described an incident in World War II, in which the skipper of a damaged bomber refused to bail out and abandon a wounded comrade. 'Go ahead,' he told the crew. 'Jump. I'm staying here and riding down with the kid.' It concluded: 'In our book, Sammy Reshevsky made such a decision back in August when, against his better judgment, he decided to play in this tournament ... knowing that his best efforts were foredoomed to failure, he "rode down" ... with no hope of anything other than the maintenance of his own self-respect, and the satisfaction of knowing that he had done his best for American chess. For this he will get no medals, and no songs will be sung about him, for anything other than first place in a tournament like this is like yesterday's newspaper. He is, of course, bitterly disappointed over his failure to achieve the impossible. All Americans should help lighten his load by paying tribute to the nerve and fighting spirit of Sammy Reshevsky.' ∎

As the Zurich chess fans watch their every move, Levon Aronian and Vladimir Kramnik agree to disagree in a lively postmortem.

At the venerable age of 203 years, the Zurich chess club continues to add memorable events to its rich history. With the financial support of Russian businessman and ardent chess lover Oleg Skvortsov, the oldest chess club in the world staged a friendly match between Vladimir Kramnik and Levon Aronian at the opulent Hotel Savoy Baur en Ville in the financial heart of Zurich. Unfettered by high stakes the players treated their fans to lively games. **Yannick Pelletier**, one of the match commentators, reports.

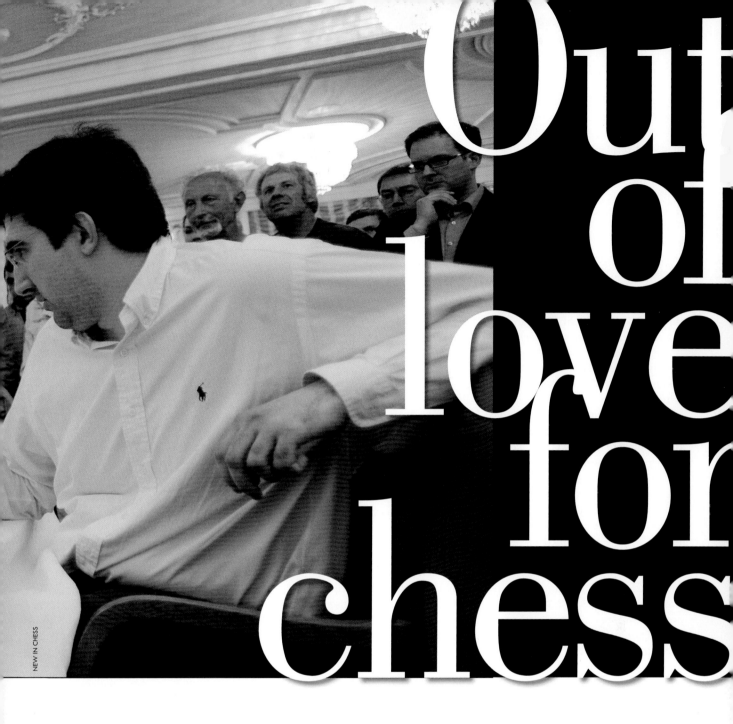

Out of love for chess

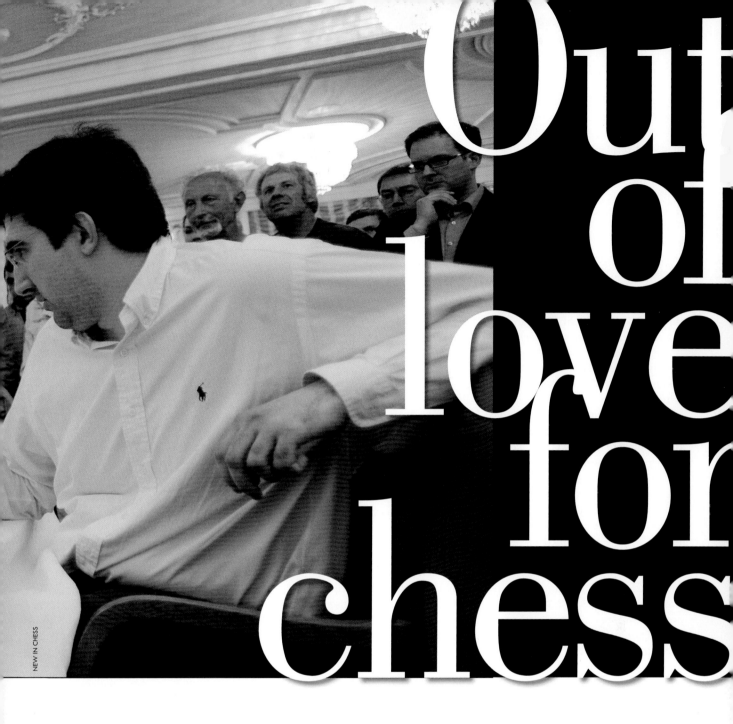

NEW IN CHESS

Around the end of January, news was spreading that Vladimir Kramnik was going to play a six-game match against Levon Aronian. For these serious pretenders for the world title this training encounter would be a valuable test for the upcoming Candidates' tournament, which at that point had not yet been postponed till March 2013. The man behind the idea was a Russian businessman named Oleg Skvortsov. These days, this soft-spoken Russian is known as the General Director of diamond company IGC. However, chess players of his generation may remember him as a young Candidate Master who left chess about 25 years ago in order to build up his business. It must be a thrilling life to rise to such an important post and have so many responsibilities. One may easily be absorbed by all this work and forget about everything else, including the passion of your younger years. Not so Oleg Skvortsov! After all these years he decided to come back to the chess world and finance a match for Russia's current number one, Vladimir Kramnik.

Perhaps more than a sponsor, we should see Skvortsov as a patron. After all, even though he managed to involve some of his business partners from Antwerp, he does not expect to gain publicity from this match. As he readily admitted, the diamond market is a very closed world, whose clientele are reliable but hard to attract.

Having decided to stage a match, Skvortsov asked Vladimir Kramnik in which city he would like to play. Antwerp seemed like a logical choice, but instead, Kramnik immediately indicated the Savoy in Zurich as his favourite venue. Having played there on several occasions – like many other champions – he obviously has a weak spot for this high-class and elegant hotel situated in the centre of the largest Swiss city. Now only the Schachgesellschaft Zürich had to be talked into providing the infrastructure and taking care of all organizational details. The oldest chess club in the world (see the report by Vladimir Kramnik(!)in New In Chess 2009/7 on the 200th anniversary of the club, which attracted a fair number of World Champions) did not need long to find a few local partners to take care of this unique event. Within weeks everything had been settled.

Was it because of this wonderful setting that Skvortsov stayed in Zurich for the duration of the event? That certainly helped. But the main reason why he abandoned his work for no fewer than 10 days was his love of chess. Not only did he eagerly follow all the games, exchanging opinions about moves, strategies, the contenders' state of mind and anything related to chess, he also sat at the board himself and played a few friendly and private games with both top players, as well as some other grandmasters, including living legend Viktor Kortchnoi. There too, his passion for the game could be readily felt.

For the two champions, playing under such circumstances was a pleasure. The only fear the spectators might have had was that they might relax and compete without the necessary tension. After all, they both left trainers and seconds at home and travelled to Zurich with loved ones. The Berlin-based Armenian came with his parents, while Kramnik was accompanied by his wife and daughter. At the opening ceremony, the charming 3-year-old Daria was responsible for

the drawing of lots. No doubt, she's been educated well. She immediately picked the right box of Swiss chocolates – the white pieces in daddy's first game!

For this encounter Aronian appeared completely focused, and he exploited a hole in Kramnik's opening preparation. The Russian ended up under pressure, defended poorly and lost.

SL 6.9 – D43
Vladimir Kramnik
Levon Aronian
Zurich 2012 (1)
1.♘f3 d5 2.d4 ♘f6 3.c4 c6 4.♘c3 e6

Aronian had been very successful with the Orthodox QG in Wijk aan Zee, but for this match he relied on the Semi-Slav. Incidentally, this was also Anand's choice in his World Championship match against Kramnik in 2008, when the Indian won the title.
5.♗g5 h6 6.♗xf6 ♕xf6 7.e3 ♘d7 8.♗d3 dxc4 9.♗xc4 g6 10.0-0 ♗g7

11.♖e1 0-0 12.e4 e5 13.d5 ♖d8
This idea may well dissuade White from playing 11.♖e1 in the future.

14.♖e3
14.h3 should be preferred here, as the rook will now be useless on e3.
14...b5 15.dxc6 bxc4 16.♘d5

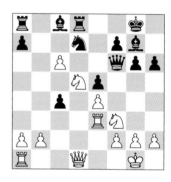

16...♕e6
In the decisive game of the recent European Women's Championship between Gunina and Muzychuk (see New In Chess 2012/3 – ed.), Black went for 16...♕d6?!, but was gradually outplayed after 17.cxd7 ♗xd7 18.♘d2 ♗b5?! 19.♕c2. The d6-square is not very natural for the queen, and computer programs instantly suggest Aronian's novelty as an improvement. As Kramnik admitted at the press conference, he had 'browsed through this game quickly but forgotten to check it with an engine'. This mistake would cost him dearly. He sank into thought and understood that he would have to fight for equality.
17.cxd7 ♖xd7 18.♕a4
As said, White has an unpleasant choice to make between slightly inferior continuations, e.g. 18.♘d2 ♗b7 19.♘xc4 ♗xd5 20.exd5 ♖xd5, followed by ...f5.
Possibly more resilient was 18.b3 cxb3 19.♕xb3 – Black remains slightly

better thanks to his two bishops, but White can pin his hopes on his strong ♘d5.

18...♗b7 19.♕xc4

19...♗xd5 At the press conference, Aronian explained why he preferred swapping immediately on d5 instead of playing the obvious 19...♖c8, which seems to gain a tempo. He generally assessed his chances as better in an endgame than with the queens still on the board. And thus, by taking on d5 immediately, he decided to invite his opponent to swap queens in the process. Yet 19...♖c8 is objectively quite strong, as after 20.♕e2 ♗xd5 21.exd5 ♖xd5 Black controls both open files and enjoys the greater activity.

20.exd5 ♕xd5 21.♕xd5 ♖xd5 22.♖ae1 After 22.♖c1 f5 White will have trouble stopping the advance of the e-pawn.

22...♖e8 23.g4 ♔h7

Kramnik's last move was useful, as 23...f5 would allow 24.♘h4, when both f5 and g6 are being hit.

24.g5?!

Quite an interesting moment. The human eye does not like such a move, which destroys the pawn structure,

Oleg Skvortsov, General Director of diamond company IGC, has not forgotten about his old love and seems more passionate about chess than ever.

but the computer does not mind, and even believes this to be the best move. Unfortunately for Kramnik, he failed to follow through and played too 'humanly'. During our live comments, Werner Hug and I believed that White should try to transfer his knight to c4: 24.♖3e2 f5 25.gxf5 gxf5 26.♘d2 e4 27.♘c4, where it will be supported by b3 and contribute to impeding the advance of Black's central pawns.

24...hxg5 25.♘xg5+ ♔g8

26.f4?

Houdini justifies 24.g5 by following up with 26.♖a3 ♖e7 (26...f6 27.♘e4 f5 28.♘g5 ♗f6 29.♖a6 won't do the trick for Black) 27.♖c3, when White will certainly get some activity. But how long will it compensate for the structural damage?

26...♖b8

Aronian keeps things simple by

removing his rook from the e-file. 26...♖d4 was also possible.

27.fxe5 27.b3 exf4 28.♖e8+ ♖xe8 29.♖xe8+ ♗f8 looks hopeless.

27...♖xb2 28.♘f3 Kramnik prefers to shed a pawn to prevent the intrusion on the second rank. Indeed, after 28.a3 ♖dd2 29.♘f3 ♖g2+ 30.♔h1 Black plays 30...♖gf2! to prevent 31. e6. He will then improve the position of his bishop and create new threats.

28...♖xa2 29.e6 fxe6 30.♖xe6 ♖f5 31.♘h4

31...♖f4! Good technique! White cannot take the pawn.

32.♖6e4

32.♘xg6? fails to 32...♗d4+ 33.♔h1 ♖ff2, when the mating threat on h2 cannot be parried satisfactorily.

32...♖f6!?

This moment was scrutinized during the press conference. It is interesting to note that opinions diverged. Kramnik believed that Black would be able to convert his pawn advantage quite easily after swapping a rook pair. And it's true that it isn't hard to be optimistic when you're looking from the black side of the board! But Aronian said that he did not feel confident enough. He preferred to keep all four rooks on the board in order to harass the white king.

The continuation 32...♖xe4 33.♖xe4 ♔f7 34.♖c4 would not be the most accurate, as Black would still need good technique.

32...♖a4! would have been a better way to swap rooks. After 33.♖xa4 (33. ♖xf4 ♖xf4 would force White to play the ugly 34.♘g2) 33...♖xa4 34.♘f3 Black also swaps the second rook with 34...♖a1, after which the win is trivial.

33.♖g4 ♔f7 34.♖c1 ♗h6 35. ♖c7+ ♔e8 36.♖e4+

White's activity soon evaporates.

36...♔d8

37.♖h7?!

A logical move, but withdrawing the rook was the lesser evil.

37...♗f8! 38.♖d4+ ♔c8 39.♖c4+ ♔b8

40.♖d7? With only two minutes left, Kramnik goes astray. But even after the more tenacious 40.♖c1 a5 Black's victory would only be a matter of time.

40...g5 41.♘g6 ♗d6

White resigned. He will either lose the knight or get mated after 42...♗xh2+ and 43...♖f1.

After this shocker, Aronian used the momentum to surprise his opponent right from the start of the second game: 1.e4! He pressed a bit in a Berlin Defence but Kramnik defended well and held the draw. For some reason, I had the impression that Kramnik had not prepared very thoroughly for this match. And in a way Aronian's decision to gain experience in open positions as White rather helped his opponent, who could play on 'auto-pilot' in the Berlin. As a consequence, Kramnik hardly suffered with black. I'm not claiming that obtaining an advantage against this super-solid champion is easy, but one might have expected Aronian to exert more pressure from the opening.

The third game was undoubtedly the most complicated and captivating one of the match.

NOTES BY
Vladimir Kramnik

SO 3.1 – C47
**Vladimir Kramnik
Levon Aronian**
Zurich 2012 (3)

1.e4 The last time I played 1.e4 in a classical game was in 2006. Since this was a training match, we were both trying something new and we both played 1.e4.

1...e5 2.♘f3 ♘c6 3.♘c3 ♘f6 4.d4 exd4 5.♘xd4

This line is considered quite drawish, but I had some ideas. I was looking at it from the black side and there was a set-up for White that was not so easy to deal with. But after only a brief think Levon played:

5...♗c5

This was his general strategy in this match. If he ran into something unexpected, he very quickly moved away from what he thought was my preparation.

This happened here, too, with the text-move, although I believe that

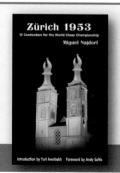

objectively speaking 5...♗b4 is a safer and better move. But I had done some work on 5...♗c5, too.

6.♗e3 ♗b6

7.♕d2 This is what I had planned to play in case he'd go ...♗c5.

Of course, the most principled move is 7.♘xc6, and now the theory goes 7...bxc6 8.e5 ♗xe3 (Black's play is pretty forced) 9.fxe3 ♘d5 10.♘xd5 cxd5 11.♕xd5 ♕h4+ 12.♔d1 (there is no choice, as after 12.g3 Black plays 12...♕b4+) 12...♖b8. There were quite a few games with this position and things seem to be unclear. Black definitely has some compensation for the pawn. So I decided to play the most logical set-up with ♕d2 and castling on opposite wings.

7...0-0 8.0-0-0 ♖e8 9.f3

The structure with opposite castling is pretty standard and it is known that if Black doesn't hurry with a break in the centre he will end up in a difficult position.

9...d5

After, for instance, 9...d6 I play 10.g4, forever stopping ...d5, and then start to push my kingside pawns, and it is clear that Black hasn't managed to

solve his opening problems at all. All Black's previous play only makes sense if he goes ...d5.

10.exd5 10.♗b5 looks tempting, but doesn't seem to yield anything after 10...♗d7 11.♘xc6 ♗xc6, when Black seems to be OK.

10...♘xd5 11.♗g5!

This was the end of my preparation. I didn't study every subvariation, but I saw that the computer gave the position after 11.♗g5 as slightly better for White. But I didn't look at the lines that were given, and here I was totally on my own. The big question was whether Levon was out of his book here or not. On the one hand, the sacrifice he went for now looked quite suspect, on the other hand, he played his next moves quickly, which usually tells one of two things: that he was still following his preparation or that he was incredibly confident.

As for myself, even if this had been my preparation, I would have taken at least 20 minutes to recheck each and every line – you're sacrificing a queen, after all. But he played his next move after just a five-minute think, leaving everyone, including myself, guessing.

11...♘xc3

A safer way to play was 11...f6, which should be tenable for Black. The line is pretty forced now: 12.♗c4 ♘xd4 13.♘xd5 ♗e6 (most of these moves are only moves, especially Black's) 14.♗xf6 gxf6 15.♘xb6 axb6 16.♕xd4 ♕xd4 17.♗xe6+ ♖xe6 18.♖xd4 ♖xa2 19.♔b1 ♖a5 20.♖d7, and it is clear that this is no picnic for Black – he is still suffering, but he should be able to make a draw.

I believe that Levon had generally decided to make matters as complicated as possible in this match. At least that was the feeling I got from his opening choices, particularly as Black, and his aggressive play. It didn't work too well for him, and after the match he said that he regretted his approach and expressed the opinion that perhaps he had been a bit too aggressive and that this had backfired, particularly in this game.

In the end I think his queen sacrifice was a strategic decision. He didn't want to end up in a worse endgame and decided to go for complications. Another part of the explanation may be that he may have slightly overestimated his position.

12.♗xd8 ♘xd1

13.♗xc7

My first thought after he played 11...♘xc3 was that maybe I had missed something, but then I remembered that the computer indicated that the position was slightly better for White, and this was reassuring – I could not be completely lost.

Here, for the first time in the game, I took some time and decided to go for this continuation, which is the only possible way to go for a win.

Actually, White is quite safe after 13.♗h4 ♘xd4 14.♕xd1 ♘f5 15.♗g5 h6, although my first thought was that Black still has some initiative and that even if I managed to defuse it, it would still be very difficult to win this position.

13...♗xc7 14.♘xc6 ♘e3

The only move, but now the situation becomes really tense.

15.♗b5!

This is clearly the best move, because there is nothing better.

15.♘b4 is not really an option, as after 15...♗f4 16.♘d3 ♗h6 17.f4 ♗f5 18.♔b1 ♖ac8 Black has a strong initiative.

15...bxc6

I also looked at the line that many commentators believed to be the best option, but I could not believe that Levon sacrificed his queen to go for this line: 15...♗f5 16.♘d4 ♗f4 17. ♗xe8 ♘xg2 18.♕xf4 ♘xf4 19.♗xf7+ ♔xf7 20.♘xf5 ♖d8 21.b3, and Black is a pawn down. He does have drawing chances but he still has a long way to go.

Another option was 15...a6 16.♗a4, and it took me some time to see whether this would made a real difference, but even if it had, it would have been in White's favour.

Finally, 15...♗f4 was tempting, but it simply loses to 16.♘e7+! ♔f8 17.g3.

16.♗xc6

16...♘c4

This was a critical position. As we found out at the press conference, Levon and I had very different opin-

ions about the position. It was clear to me that the only way to challenge White was to play 16...♗f4. It took me quite some time to calculate all variations to the very end, because the position is so full of tricks: 17.♗b1 (the only move, as after 17.♖e1 ♗b7! the game is over, because now Black not only threatens the simple 18... ♘xg2, but also the beautiful 18... ♘c4, which is winning on the spot because of the mate on e1) 17...♗f5 looks frightening, but after 18.♗xa8! (I checked this at least three times. It was good old Alexander Kotov who wrote a book about how to calculate variations – translated into English as *Think Like A Grandmaster*, ed. – and gave the advice that you should calculate any variation only once. I am not so sure that Mr Kotov would check these variations only once either. So I checked them several times and was happy to see that the computer confirmed my calculations after the game) 18...♖xa8 (after 18...♘xc2 I have 19.♕xf4; if 18...♘xc2+ 19.♔a1 ♗g6 I have 20.♗e4) 19.♖e1! ♗xc2+ (19...♘xc2 20.♕xf4 ♘a3+ 21.♔c1) 20.♔a1 ♖e8 21.g3, which is the move that the computer says is winning (I stopped my calculations after seeing 21.♖xe3).

So after a long think Levon played 16...♘c4, admitting that the queen sacrifice had not been a great success. I was quite surprised to hear after the game that he thought that he was better here.

17.♕d4

I felt that I was clearly better, but I was disappointed about this move,

which makes everything less simple. I had seen and was planning to play 17.♕b4!, which would have led to a serious advantage for White, but after 17...♗e6 I mainly considered 18. ♗xa8, which looks strong. But clearly stronger is 18.♗xe8. The computer, as usual, plays for tricks and, as usual, it is right: 18...♖xe8 19.♖e1!. A very strong move, which I had missed, as now, after 19...♗a5 and 20.♖xe6, everything is going to work.

17...♗e6 18.♗xa8

18...♗b6!

I don't recall exactly whether I had half missed this strong move or underestimated it, but I was unpleasantly surprised by it, since it disrupts the coordination of my pieces.

19.♕d3

I believed that I could play 19.♕e4 here, but after 19...♗e3+ Black has at least a draw: 20.♔d1 (as I cannot go to b1 because of the fork on d2) 20... ♘xb2+ 21.♔e1 ♗d7 22.♕b7 ♗b6+ 23.♔d2 ♗e3+ 24.♔e2.

19...♖xa8

Levon was quite seriously considering playing 19...♖d8, when I had planned 20.♕xd8+ (he rejected it

because of 20.♗d5 ♖xd5 21.♕xc4
♖d1+ 22.♖xd1 ♗xc4 23.b3, thinking
White was better. I agree with him,
but I am not so sure that this is easy
to win) 20...♗xd8 21.g3 (to stop all
kinds of checks) 21...♗b6 22.b3 ♘e3
23.c3, and I think this position should
be better for me in the long run. I will
slowly start pushing my pawns, and
although Black will probably be able
to hold, it will be no fun.

A strange position has arisen. Levon
was afraid of 20.b3, because he didn't
see anything better than 20...♖d8 21.
bxc4 ♖xd3 22.cxd3 ♔f8 23.♔c2 ♗d4,
and it's pretty drawish.
My thinking was quite different. I was
afraid to play 20.b3, because I thought
it was very drawish and I was still
playing for a win. During the game
our assessments were very different,
but after analysing the position carefully I still believe that it is White who
is better here and that Black is fighting
for a draw.
Still, queen against three pieces is
one of the most difficult balances
to assess in chess. A lot depends on
the concrete positions of the pieces,
how active they are and how solidly
they are positioned. These are always
difficult to assess because they are
dynamic matters.
I can understand someone believing
that Black is better here. Suppose he
can play his bishop from b6 to f6 without doing any damage, then I would
agree that he is not worse at all. But
this is far from easy.
20.♖e1 ♖d8 21.♕e4 My assessment during the game was that everything would be clarified by the

As Vladimir Kramnik's daughter Daria offers her father a well-deserved
drink, his wife Marie-Laure takes photos for the family album.

next two, three moves. If Black failed
to create some threats soon, I would
have good winning chances. Perhaps
he had some tricks or could keep an
initiative. Having analysed the position, I have come to the conclusion
that there are no such black tricks and
that White is significantly better.
Levon's next move came as quite a surprise both to me and to the spectators.
Perhaps he was still playing for a win,
or perhaps he was having his doubts
and was looking for ways to save the
game.

21...g5?! The point of this move is
easy to see, as f4 is a very good square
for White. I would be happy to put my
queen there. Levon prevents this and
maybe hopes to get his bishop there at
some stage. But the price Black is paying is too high: he opens up his king
and offers White a clear target.

I also examined 21...♖d4 (to disturb the centralized queen) 22.♕c6
♖d8, but then I found 23.♖xe6!, an
important theme in this position: the
moment I give back the exchange, all
Black's pieces lose their coordination:
23...fxe6 24.♕xe6+ ♔f8 (obviously
I cannot take the knight because of
...♗e3+ and mate) 25.a4 ♘e3 26.♔b1,
and I am ready to start pushing my
pawns: 26...♘xg2 27.a5 ♗e3 28.c4,
and Black's position is very difficult.
Materially he is almost equal, but he
cannot coordinate his pieces. When
I start pushing my pawns, he'll be hard
put to survive.
But it was better to play 21...g6, or
21...h6, that's a matter of taste, when
in both cases I was intending to continue 22.c3, followed by ♕f4, threatening ♖xe6, when I believe White still
has an advantage.
22.c3
An important prophylactic move.
22...♗c5
Around this time Levon was also
getting into time-trouble. I still had
about 20 minutes, he about 10. And
whatever Black does, he has to watch
out for so many tricks. For instance,
if you want to transfer your bishop
via f8 to g7, which would be a logical
plan, you'd have to reckon with ♕c6
and suddenly all your pieces are hang-

ing. Black has too many pieces to take care of.

23.♖e2 I didn't want to hurry, but according to the computer I could already start with 23.h4, which it thinks is very powerful. The text is the human move, protecting against ...♖d2 etc., and I played it very quickly.

23...h6 24.g3

Again no hurry. Asking Black what is his plan. My general plan is to go f4.

24...a5 Black has to create some play on the queenside.

25.f4 a4

26.f5!

After some thinking I went for this principled advance.

The computer also likes 26.h4 a3 27. b4, but it doesn't look very human to me to leave the knight on c4.

26...♗d5 27.♕d3

The position is difficult for Black; it's so easy to drop a piece.

27...♗b6 28.b3!

Now I start attacking Black's pieces with every move. The only 'risk' is that my king will be a bit exposed.

28...axb3 29.axb3 ♘a5

30.♖e8+

An interesting moment in the game. This is the human solution to the position, and I think that if I were to play this position again I'd still go for it, as it clarifies matters.

The computer recommends more adventurous ways of playing, such as 30.b4!? ♘c4 31.f6 ♗e6 32.♕f3, and its assessment is much better for White. But close to real time-trouble this is not the way you play.

And it says that a clear win is 30.♕b5, a move that I had seen. But things are

far less clear after 30...♘xb3+ 31.♔c2, and now suddenly 31...♘d4+ 32.cxd4 ♗xd4, and it is quite possible that this will end in some sort of fortress. There is a famous game between Polugaevsky and Geller (Skopje 1968) which is very similar: three pawns against three pawns and queen against two bishops on one flank (because the rooks will probably be exchanged).

30...♖xe8 31.♕xd5

White runs no risk of losing at all, whereas Black has serious problems with the coordination of his pieces. As my opponent admitted after the game, Black may objectively have chances to save the game, but in a practical game it is almost impossible.

31...♖d8 32.♕b5 ♖d6 33.♔c2!

An important move, stopping ...♘c6. It would be a mistake to hurry and start pushing my pawns, for after 33. b4 ♗e3+ 34.♔c2 ♘c6 Black all of a sudden gets some coordination.

33...♔g7

Down to one minute, Levon commits the decisive mistake.

After the game the computer showed that the only way to stay in the game was 33...♗d8, when the most logical line runs 34.♕e8+ ♔g7 35.♕e5+ ♖f6 36.b4 ♘c6 37.♕e4 ♗c7 38.b5 ♘e5 39. c4, and it is clear that White is pressing, but Black definitely has drawing chances.

34.b4

Now, with precise play (I was mostly playing the first choice of the computer), White wins.

34...♘b7 35.c4!

Exploiting the loose positions of the black pieces.

35...♖f6 36.g4

Probably the most exact and certainly the most unpleasant move for Black if you only have something like 20 seconds left.

36...♘d8 37.c5 ♗c7 38.♕d7

It's already clear that Black is dropping material.

38...♘c6 39.b5 ♘a7 40.♕xc7 ♘xb5 41.♕e5

Again the human approach. The computer shows a forced win with 41.♕d7 ♘c6 42.f6+ ♔g6 43.♕d3+ ♔xf6 44.♕xb5. But I didn't even want to think about such things, as 41.♕e5 is a very simple win.

41...♘a7 42.♔d3

And Levon took one or two minutes to cool down before resigning. There is no way to save the game with the pinned rook.

I felt that it was a good game, at least on my part. After my slightly shaky start it gave me confidence. And according to the spectators, it was the most entertaining game in the match.

■ ■ ■

The tournament's regulations stipulated that if a game ended in a draw within three hours, a rapid game would have to be played right afterwards, the outcome of which would not count for the overall result. The aim of this special rule was to compensate the spectators for the 'premature' draw and offer them an additional game for the show. This happened only on the fourth day, when Aronian bumped against the Berlin Wall and made a draw after about one and a half hours. If the aim was to please the crowd afterwards, both players completely fulfilled this task. Kramnik sacrificed some central pawns in order to launch an attack, but Aronian calculated better and countered with apparent ease.

Both final encounters featured hard-fought draws and so the match ended in a 3-3 tie, which looked like a fair result. At the final press conference, Kramnik explained that he was quite happy with the quality of the games except for the first round. Aronian, on his part, felt this match had been a very useful experience for him.

Both players expressed their gratitude toward the sponsor, the organizers and the spectators. Indeed, Zurich has a long tradition of great chess events. The local crowd is made up of connoisseurs and all games drew a full house both on working days and in the weekend. English comments were provided both for them and on livestream videos.

I believe that Oleg Skvortsov thoroughly enjoyed his stay in Zurich and the whole atmosphere around the match. And so did everyone else! Let us hope for a 'bis repetita!' ■

Zurich 2012 match			1	2	3	4	5	6		TPR
Vladimir Kramnik	IGM RUS	2801	0	½	1	½	½	½	3	2820
Levon Aronian	IGM ARM	2820	1	½	0	½	½	½	3	2801

The stylish Hipp Theatre in the centre of Malmö, 'only two minutes away from the players' hotel, a detail most people would consider irrelevant, but that the spoilt and lazy chess players find important.'

T

This year the Sigeman tournament celebrated its 20th edition, something unimaginable for me, who had not been born until a couple of editions had passed. Yet I have quite a good idea of what the tournament is about, as I was invited for the third consecutive time and had been wandering around the streets of Malmö. The tournament is played in a beautiful hall that may have been a ballroom of some Danish king some centuries ago (unfortunately, your narrator is not well versed in history), a beautiful chamber full of mirrors and classical decorations, only two minutes away from the players' hotel, a detail most people would consider irrelevant, but that the spoilt and lazy chess players find important.

To celebrate the jubilee edition, the organizers expanded the field on both ends, so to speak, as they invited one more foreign player and one more Swedish one, making it an eight-player top event, and if I am not mistaken, the strongest so far in its history, at least according to average rating. Alongside me, the foreign contingent consisted of Peter Leko, Fabiano Caruana and Li Chao, while Sweden was represented by Nils Grandelius, Emanuel Berg, Hans Tikkanen and Jonny Hector.

The opening ceremony was a lively occasion, starring a famous Swedish singer and a delicious meal to enjoy the singing with. The only upsetting fact was that I took the bottom number, number 8, getting an extra

More good memories from Malmö

A chess player can consider himself lucky if there is an amazing tournament he is invited to play in every year. One such player is me and one such amazing tournament is a world-class event in Malmö, named after its main sponsor and organizer, the law firm Sigeman & Co.

Anish Giri

black game. But then again, the white advantage, if handled by a well-prepared opponent, has been proven to be a deceptive psychological effect (which allowed me to score yet another two surprisingly easy black wins).

Fabiano Caruana, who was comfortably the first seed in the event thanks to his imperial 2770 rating, was not really a surprise winner of this jubilee edition, yet here and there things could have gone quite differently. But, well, we will get there...

I myself was struggling to fight for top place after rather unnecessarily (to put it mildly) losing to Fabiano in the first round. Remarkably enough, when there were six ways to protect a pawn so as not to have to worry about

First seed Fabiano Caruana lived up to expectations, but it wasn't an easy ride.

the future, I chose the seventh one, provoking tactics which turned out to be in my opponent's favour.

Caruana-Giri
position after 32.♕a4

32...♗d6??
Let's count. So ...♗d8, ...♗d7, ...♗b8, ...♕d7, ...♕e8, ...♕a8.., all of

them would have kept the position unchanged and equal.

33.♘c4! I wanted to provoke 33.♗c4, after which I equalize by force with 33...b5 34.♗xe6 ♘xe6 35.♕a2 ♘c7!. The text-move I thought was impossible, as I had missed the simple 35.♕d1 from a distance.

33...♗xc4? Now I totally collapsed. Things went from bad to worse.

After 33...♗b8 White plays 34.♘xb6!. But 33...b5! would have given me a good chance to save the game after 34.♘xd6 bxa4 35.♘xc8 ♗xc8 36.♗xa7 a3, when suddenly *my* a-pawn turns into a force for a while: 37.♗c4! ♗xa6 38.♗a2 ♗e2! A very important detail. 39.♗e3 ♘h7 40.♔g2 g5, and Black gets counterplay, maybe even enough to save the game.

34.♗xc4 b5? 35.♕d1!

35...♗e7? I played my moves out of inertia, missing that the queen from d1 is going to the kingside.

36.♗b3 ♘e6 37.♕g4 ♗f8 38.♕f5 ♗f6 39.g4 ♔e8 40.g5 hxg5 41. hxg5 Black resigned.

After this game I never came close to the lead, but fortunately I somewhat consolidated my tournament and managed to play a few reasonable games and be content with them, a feeling I have been missing lately. Still, I must admit that my two black wins, in which my opponents Tikkanen and Berg definitely underperformed, weren't something I could be remarkably proud of. But a win is a win and the more of them the better. In my white games I somehow failed to impress from start to finish, although

I must say I did waste a nice advantage against both Li Chao and Jonny Hector.

I was lucky to have caused Peter Leko too many worries and Berlin Wall nightmares before our game and so already before the game I sort of got away from him. As Peter told me afterwards, he had been in a state of panic and in the end even discarded the Anti-Berlin as too theoretical, going for the quiet Italian Opening instead. Remembering my sleepless nights preparing for an Italian duel with French top GM Etienne Bacrot half a year ago (which I did win after all), I quickly threw in a couple of moves and soon the drawish vibes around our board got too close for Peter to fight against.

Nowadays, the opening plays a big role in such strong events, and indeed there were a couple of drawn

> 'I am eagerly waiting for the mysterious Chinese small bottle of oil he promised me at the closing ceremony'

but highly theoretical games, like the one in which Peter Leko got hit by an amazing blow from Grandelius, that was good enough to save the draw for the Swede.

My game against Leko was played after his clash with Nils, and in the end a desperate Peter, who came to Malmö to 'just play chess', threw in 1.d4 against Berg and crushed him in his healthy positional style. At the finish Leko almost managed to catch Fabiano, but it wasn't meant to be. After escaping against Li Chao and then

having luck again on his side against Grandelius, Fabiano rolled over Jonny Hector, clinching an incredible +4 in just seven rounds.

Among the Swedish players, it was definitely Nils Grandelius who stood out. He was even fighting for first place in the penultimate round.

Caruana-Grandelius
position after 29.♕xc6

29...axb2?
After an absolutely random beginning a complicated game arose, but here, in time-trouble, Nils had a chance to affect the outcome of the tournament. Instead of the pawn capture, he could have played 29...♕a5!!, and suddenly Black is winning: 30.bxa3 ♖fc8! 31.♕d6 ♕xa4 32.♖f1 ♕a7, and the queen is trapped.

30.♕c2 ♕a5 31.f4 ♖fc8 32. ♘c5 ♕b4 33.♕b1 ♕c3 34.♔g2 ♖xc5!? 35.dxc5 ♖b3 36.♖f1

36...♖a3?
And here he could have played 36...♗e7!!, and Black is still in the game, even though he is a rook down: 37.f5 ♗xc5 38.fxe6 fxe6 39.♕g6 ♕d2+ 40.♔h1 b1♕ 41.♖xb1 ♖xb1+

Among the Swedish players, it was definitely Nils Grandelius who stood out.

42.♕xb1 ♕e3 – a brilliant, study-like draw.
37.♖f2! ♖a1 38.♕xb2 ♕e1 39. ♖h5 g6 40.fxg5 gxh5 41.♕b8+ ♔g7 42.♖xf7+ Black resigned.

The other Swedish players seemed to play two events, one before the rest day, when we went out to watch the exciting handball final of the Swedish league, and one after it. Berg and Hector played the first event well and collapsed in the second one, while Hans Tikkanen performed the other way around, managing to recover from a painful streak of four zeros.

Li Chao, who collapsed after experiencing another miracle performed by Fabiano, won't be too content either with his final result. However, I was delighted to see Li staying friendly and truthful to his positive mood up to the very end, and I am eagerly waiting for the mysterious Chinese small bottle of oil he promised me at the closing ceremony (yes, Li, now your promise is documented).

That closing ceremony took place in a quiet restaurant with just a few guests and was a warm and pleasant way to end yet another successful Sigeman & Co chess tournament. Endless and fascinating stories told by Peter Leko kept the evening going for

a long time and at the end I would bet anyone that all of us were delighted with this wonderful event and left Malmö hoping to come back!

NOTES BY
Fabiano Caruana

GI 4.16 – D85
**Li Chao
Fabiano Caruana**
Malmö 2012 (5)

1.d4 ♘f6 2.♘f3 g6 3.c4 ♗g7 4. ♘c3 d5 5.cxd5 ♘xd5 6.e4 ♘xc3 7.bxc3 c5 8.♖b1 0-0 9.♗e2

9...♘c6
An uncommon and risky move. I wanted to avoid the main line, which the theory considers adequate for

equality but often leads to drawish positions.
10.d5 ♘e5 11.♘xe5 ♗xe5 12.♕d2 e6 13.f4

13...♗c7 A further risky continuation. The dark-squared bishop abandons the defence of the kingside in order to prevent the advance of White's c-pawn from a5.
13...♗g7 14.c4 is considered by the theory to be better for White.
14.0-0
Now 14.c4?? is impossible, of course, due to 14...♗a5.
14...exd5 15.exd5 ♗a5 16.d6 ♖b8

17.♖b5
An interesting exchange sacrifice. In some lines, White prepares to sacrifice on a5, which is necessary in order for him to be able to play f5.
Previously I had faced 17.♗b2 b5 18. ♖bd1 ♗d7 19.♗f3 c4, and once Black fixes the pawn on c3 he is usually OK. I eventually won a complicated game against Yannick Pelletier.
17...♗d7
I had analysed this position a few years ago, but could only vaguely remember how Black is supposed to

play. However, my next few moves are correct.

18.f5! A strong move. White will soon be attacking with all his pieces, while Black has limited resources to organize an efficient defence.

Another possibility is 18.♖xa5 ♕xa5 19.f5, but Black achieves equality with 19...c4! 20.f6 ♕c5+ 21.♔h1 ♔h8 22.♕h6 ♖g8 23.♗g5 ♕e5 24.♗xc4 ♗c6 25.♗xf7 ♕e2 26.♖g1 ♗g2+ 27.♖xg2 ♕f1+, with a draw.

18...♗xb5

18...♗xf5? 19.♖xf5 gxf5 20.♖xa5 is

the point behind 17.♖b5. Black is mated after 20...♕xa5 21.♕g5+ ♔h8 22.♕f6+ ♔g8 23.♗h6.

19.♗xb5

19...♕h4

Preventing White's queen from invading h6, but my queen is liable to be kicked around on the kingside. The position is starting to get very sharp, and any mistake by either side will be severely punished. White has to act fast, before Black plays ...♖bd8, after which White will be tied to defending the d-pawn. Of course, if White

is forced to play d7, Black will take his bishop back to c7 and neutralize White's initiative.

The following variation demonstrates how dangerous Black's position is: 19...a6? 20.f6 ♗xc3 21.♕xc3 axb5 22.♕e3 ♔h8 23.♕h6 ♖g8 24.♖f3, with the threat of ♕xh7+, mating.

20.♖f4 20.g3 is met by 20...♕e4!, preparing counterplay against c3 with ...♕e5. It's important to note that once the black queen gets to the centre, Black will be fine.

20...♕g5

Since the game continuation leads to a very unpleasant position for Black, perhaps it's necessary to consider 20...♕h6!? which, in some lines, opens up the possibility of ...g5.

21.♕e1 White prepares a discovered attack with ♖f3 or ♖a4. Now Black has many options, and in all cases the position is highly dangerous for him.

21...♕d8?!
Objectively speaking, this is a decisive mistake, although the refutation is not at all obvious. However, other moves wouldn't offer much respite either.
21...a6 is met by the powerful 22.fxg6! (22.♗c4 ♖be8 gives Black counterplay) 22...♕xg6 23.♗d7! ♔h8 24.♗f5, with a strong and probably unstoppable attack.

22.♕e5
22.fxg6 would be premature: 22...hxg6 23.♕e5 ♖e8 24.♕d5 ♖e1+ 25.♔f2, and here, as opposed to the game, Black has the e6-square at his disposal: 25...♖e6!, and Black is winning.

22...♖e8 This was my idea when I played 21...♕d8. I sacrifice an exchange in order to simplify the position and head into an endgame. Unfortunately, there is a flaw:

23.♕d5!
White correctly assesses that his bishop is needed in order to attack, and is worth more than my rook. I had underestimated this move when I played 21...♕d8.
The automatic 23.♗xe8 leads to equality: 23...♕xe8 24.♕d5 (after 24.♕xe8+ ♖xe8 White's d-pawn is more a liability than an asset; 24.♕e7 ♕xe7 25.dxe7 f6 26.fxg6 hxg6 27.♖xf6 ♗xc3 28.♖xg6+ ♔f7 will yield Black reasonable chances) 24...♕c6! (an important move, forcing a queen swap; not 24...♖xc3? 25.d7 ♕e1+ 26.♖f1 ♗d4+ 27.♕xd4 ♕xf1+ 28.♔xf1 cxd4 29.♗g5, and Black loses his rook) 25.♕xc6 bxc6 26.♗e3 ♗xc3 27.♗xc5 ♗e5 28.♖a4 ♖d8, eliminating the d6-pawn, with a likely draw.

23...♖e1+ 24.♔f2

The point of White's play. The c1-bishop is a small price to pay for the attack White will get after fxg6.
24...g5 Forced. I'm trying to shore up the kingside, but it's clear that Black's king is too exposed to survive. 24...♖xc1? loses on the spot: 25.fxg6 hxg6 26.♕xf7+ ♔h8 27.♕xg6, and Black will be mated.
25.f6 h6

26.♕f5! Surprisingly enough, this is the only move. But it's a winning one. White sacrifices almost all his pieces, but it turns out that he only needs his queen and bishop to mate Black.
26.♔xe1? ♗xc3+ 27.♗d2 ♗xd2+ 28.♕xd2 gxf4 29.♕xf4 ♕a5+ can only be good for Black.

26...♕xd6 The most tenacious defence, which at least doesn't lose on the spot and forces White to make a few more accurate moves before winning. 26...♖xc1 27.♗d3, and there's no defence against ♕h7+.
26...♖d1, preventing ♗d3, fails to 27.♖g4, after which a sacrifice on g5 will win.
26...♔h8 27.♗d3 ♕g8 has many refutations, but I particularly like the following one: 28.♖f3 ♖xc1 29.♖h3 ♕g6 30.♕xg6 fxg6 31.♖xh6+ ♔g8 32.♗c4+ ♔f8 33.♖h8 mate.

27.♔xe1 ♖d8
27...♗xc3+ doesn't help much either: 28.♔e2 ♖d8 29.♗d3 (29.♖f1!? also wins) 29...♔f8 30.♕h7 ♖e8+ 31.♔f2! (other moves are less clear, but this one decides the game at once) 31...♗d4+ 32.♔f1 ♗xf6 33.♕xh6+ ♔e7 34.♖f3, and Black has no compensation for the piece.

28.♔f2??

After very powerful play Li Chao slips up and loses all his advantage. Instead, a simple move would have sufficed to win, e.g. the calm 28.♗e2! – after 28...♗xc3+ 29.♔f1 Black doesn't have enough compensation for the piece.

28...♕d1 Now White is unable to hold all his pieces together.

29.♗c4 The point is, of course, that after 29.♗e3 Black can capture 29...gxf4, and the queen on d1 protects the g4-square!

29...♔h8 30.♖f3 ♕xc1 31.♗d3 ♕d2+

Finally it all ends in a perpetual.

32.♔f1

32.♔g3?? ♕e1+ even wins for Black!

32...♕d1+ 33.♔f2 ♕d2+ 34.♔f1 ♕d1+ Draw.

After this close call, I managed to win my final two games and to become the sole winner of the tournament!

NOTES BY
Peter Leko

RE 10.3 – A13
**Hans Tikkanen
Peter Leko**
Malmö 2012 (4)

After last year's wonderful report about the 2011 Sigeman tournament (see New In Chess 2011/5), I immediately got the feeling that I should try to play there next year! I am very glad I did. Malmö is a very charming historical city, and thanks to the organizers the hotel chosen for the players has the best location in town! Right next to the walking street and the playing hall, the Hipp Theatre is just a two-minute walk. During a tournament I always like to focus only on chess, but thanks to the location in Malmö, being a chess player means you are a tourist at the same time! Every evening walk is like a sightseeing tour. The Sigeman tournament has a very big impact on Swedish chess, and it's no accident that a Swedish player is having his international breakthrough in Malmö every year. Last year it was Tikkanen, this time it was Grandelius, who played a fantastic tournament! I am already curious to see what will happen next year!

I did not start the tournament as planned, and after three rounds I had three draws, which was definitely not what I had come to Malmö for. Thanks to the rest day after the third round and a magic evening in the Malmö Arena, where the players were invited by the organizers to witness the Swedish Handball Championship Final in the ultramodern and sold out (over 12,000 spectators!!) Arena, I felt ready to start a new tournament!

1.c4 ♘f6

This was meant as a surprise. I usually react with 1...c5, but I wanted to avoid any possible preparation. I had been planning to try this for a long time, and now felt like the right moment.

2.g3 e6 3.♗g2 d5 4.♘f3 dxc4

The latest developments in this line suggest that this leads to an interesting fight for both sides, exactly what I had been looking for.

5.♕a4+ c6 6.♕xc4 b5 7.♕c2 ♗b7 8.0-0 ♘bd7 9.♘c3 There are many different move orders here. I opted for the most classical one.

9...a6 Now Black is threatening to go ...c5 immediately.

10.a4 The typical way to stop ...c5 for a while.

10...♖c8

Black prepares to meet White's d2-d4. Now it is common and sensible for White to switch plans and not to push the d-pawn two squares.

11.d3 11.d4 is nicely met by 11...b4 12.♘e4 c5!, and Black is fine.

11...♗e7 12.e4 This set-up has become very popular in the last few years, the point being that White simply gains space and expands in the centre. Without the pawn on d4 Black can't break out with ...c5, but without ...c5 it is not clear what Black should do.

12...0-0 13.h3
A useful move. White prepares ♗e3 and eagerly waits for Black to show his cards. Actually, my preparation was not very deep. Basically I relied on the feeling that I would be able to handle such a position on my own. Once we got to this position, I realized that it is far from easy to find a plan.

13...a5!
In the end I found a very interesting and original idea. Since I failed to find a good way to make ...c5 work, since without it the future of the b7-bishop looked pretty sad, I had to be creative. I did not really like 13...♕b6 because of 14.♗e3 c5 15.♖fc1 ♖fd8 16.axb5

'I can hardly recall any example of White's last move of ♘c3-b1 being met by ...♘d7-b8 in the middlegame!'

axb5 17.b4, and although I don't know if this gives him any advantage, the position is certainly much easier to play for White.

The other move that attracted my attention was 13...b4, a pretty committal move, but it also has a point: 14.♘b1 ♘c5 15.♖d1 b3 16.♕e2 (everything was pretty forced so far) 16...a5!.

ANALYSIS DIAGRAM

A similar idea as in the game. Black has given up some important squares, but after activating the bishop to a6, his activity could compensate for his positional weaknesses. It was difficult to choose between the two more or less similar options. In the end I went

for the more flexible-looking move. Somehow I still wanted to postpone ...b5-b4.

14.♖d1
White prepares to meet Black's plan.

14...♗a6 15.♗e3
White has finished his development. I had the feeling that time was on White's side, so Black has to be very energetic to prove that 13...a5 was not only an original idea but also a good one!

15...b4!
Black has to play this move anyway!

16.♘b1
Now White only needs to play ♘bd2, and Black will suffer for a long time.

16...♘b8!!
A very strong and aesthetically pleasing move! I can hardly recall any example of White's last move of ♘c3-b1 being met by ...♘d7-b8 in the middlegame! Actually, this was the main reason why I decided for 13...a5. Now White has to make some unpleasant decisions. In the meantime Black has a clear plan: play ...c5 followed by ...♘c6, and everything falls into its ideal place.

17.♗f1

Played after a long think. I had been expecting something else, but the move itself is logical. My opponent decided to ignore my plan and preferred to focus on his own possibilities. I regarded 17.♘e5 as the critical move. I had mostly been calculating this and had the following ideas:

ANALYSIS DIAGRAM

A) I did not like 17...c5, because after 18.♘d2 White gets an easy and comfortable game: 18...♘fd7 19.♘xd7 ♕xd7 20.♘b3!, and Black has some problems due to the weaknesses on a5 and c5;

B) 17...♘fd7! (this is the move!) 18.♘xd7 (now 18.♘c4 is met strongly by 18...♗xc4! 19.dxc4 ♕c7 20. ♘d2 ♗c5!, and Black is in charge) 18...♕xd7 19.d4! (this is the whole idea behind 17.♘e5), and now:

ANALYSIS DIAGRAM

19...♖fd8 is what I decided on in the end: 20.♘d2 c5! (now is the right time) 21.d5 (taking the pawn now is a different story – 21.dxc5 ♗e2! 22.♖dc1 ♗d3, and the c5-pawn will be lost sooner or later) 21...c4!, and it's obvious that Black has good counterplay.

17...c5 18.♘bd2 ♘c6

Since we both had spent a lot of time already, I decided to make this move quickly. It is a pawn sacrifice, but I can hardly imagine any human player really considering to take on c5.

19.♘b3

Also played almost instantly, and it is the logical follow-up of the plan started with 17.♗f1.

Honestly, there was no direct reason for accepting the sacrifice. It was too risky and Black is not risking anything. After 19.♗xc5 ♘d4 (19...♘d7 20.♗xe7 ♕xe7 might not be enough after 21.♖ac1) 20.♗xe7 Black should go for the forced line 20...♕xe7 21.♕b1 ♘c2 22.♖a2 b3 (I knew that I had this move, which basically forces the repetition, but I hoped that it would not be needed!) 23.♘xb3 ♘b4 24.♖a1 ♘c2 (White has no right to play for an advantage) 25. ♘xa5?! ♕b4 26.e5 ♘d7 27.♘c4 ♘xa1 28.♕xa1 ♗xc4 29.dxc4 ♘c5, which can only be better for Black.

19...♘d7

The correct decision. Black keeps the tension for the moment.

20.♖ac1

20...♘d4!

I think this was the right practical choice. We both had about 20 minutes left, which meant that we had to speed up considerably. This is why I was looking for a position that would be easier to play.

21.♗xd4 cxd4

22.♕b1?!

This came as a surprise, and quite a pleasant one, too.

I had the feeling that White had to play 22.♕d2, after which I planned to sac the d-pawn, but here White has a better coordination: 22...♘c5! 23.♘fxd4 ♕d7, with nice compensation but White can give back the pawn and get stability: 24.♘xc5 ♗xc5 25.♘f3 ♗b6! (25...♕xa4 runs into 26.d4! ♗xf1 27.dxc5 ♗xh3 28.♘e5, and suddenly Black's pieces are pretty much trapped) 26.d4 ♖xc1 27.♕xc1 ♖c8 28.♕d2 ♗b7 29.♘b5 ♕c7, also with full compensation.

22...♘c5!

Following the plan.

23.♘fxd4?

After taking the pawn White suddenly gets into serious problems. It was better to accept that Black had the initiative and play solidly with 23.♘xc5 ♗xc5 24.♘d2 ♕d7 25.b3 ♗e7 26.♖xc8 ♖xc8 27.♘c4 ♗xc4 28. dxc4, and Black is more comfortable, although it looks very drawish.

23...♕b6!
I think my opponent had forgotten about this quiet but powerful move! Now White is paralysed and has to make some ugly moves.

24.♕a2
A very sad move, as the white queen gets cut off from the game, but it was difficult to find something better. 24.♖c2 looked logical, but I spotted a nice tactical idea: 24...♘xa4 25.♖xc8 ♖xc8 26.♕a2

ANALYSIS DIAGRAM

26...♘xb2!! 27.♕xb2 a4 28.♘d2 ♖c3!, and the two pawns on the queenside connected with the powerful dark-squared bishop make White's life miserable.

24...♘xb3 First I wasn't happy about releasing the tension so quickly, but suddenly I saw a clear-cut plan.
25.♘xb3 ♗b7!
Sidestepping White's only freeing idea, d3-d4. It's very hard even to make a move for White.

Peter Leko: 'After three rounds I had three draws, which was definitely not what I had come to Malmö for.'

26.♗g2
I wasn't expecting anything else. Maybe it would have been better to exchange the rooks, but 26.♖xc8 ♖xc8 27.♕b1 ♗c6 28.♖c1 ♖c7 also feels very unpleasant. Now we see why I had taken on b3 myself. With the knight on b3, White suddenly has real problems defending the a4-pawn.
26...e5!
This is very strong! From now on White is in deep trouble. By the way, even ...♕e6 is looming, with a decisive pin!
27.♕b1
27.♖xc8 is met by 27...♗xc8!, and the bishop gets to its ideal place.
27.d4 does not work either, because after 27...exd4 White can't take back the pawn.
27...♗c6! 28.♕a1

28...♗d7! The bishop is heading for e6, and if the knight has to move from b3 then the dark-squared bishop can join the battle with ...♗c5.
29.♘d2 ♖xc1 I had a nice strategic idea and I already was too short of time to look for alternatives.
The computer likes 29...♗c5 30.♖f1 ♕h6!, but that's pretty complicated and I had no reason to go for it.
30.♖xc1 ♗c5 31.♖f1 b3!

After fixing White's weaknesses on the queenside the position is practically lost!

32.♘c4 ♕c7 33.♕d1 ♖b8

There is no need to hurry to take the a4-pawn.

34.♕h5?!

A natural human reaction. With one minute on the clock White completely loses control, but that was quite understandable.

34.♕d2 was more tenacious, but after 34...♖b4 it is also very hard to see what White can do with his extra tempo.

34...♗d4 35.♖a1 ♖b4 36.♕d1 ♕c5 37.♕d2 g6

Black's play is very simple. With every move his position improves.

38.♖c1 This loses immediately, but there was no hope anyway.

38...♖xa4 39.♘e3 ♕b4 40.♕e2 ♖a2 And after reaching the time-control, White resigned in a hopeless position.

NOTES BY
Anish Giri

VO 7.3 – A02
Emanuel Berg
Anish Giri
Malmö 2012 (7)

This game was played in the last round and we were both eager to win – Emanuel had lost his previous two games, and I had spoiled a very promising game against Hector.

Playing with black I wasn't that optimistic, knowing that I needed a bunch of luck to finally get a plus score (better late than never, as they say), but as early as move one I kind of felt that Lady Luck was finally smiling down on me.

1.f4?!

You can't imagine how delightful it is, after having tried to find an advantage for Black after 1.e4, to try to find some here. Emanuel is a principled 1.e4 player, and a player like that is often reluctant to play such offbeat and ugly-looking lines with white.

1...♘f6 2.b3

Here I realized that my opponent was aiming for a Queen's Indian with a lot of bonuses. Except for the extra tempo, the f5 push is played with-out the premature ♘e4 (I am talking about 1.d4 ♘f6 2.c4 e6 3.♘f3 b6 4.g3 ♗b7 5.♗g2, where Black often has a plan of ♘e4 f5).

However, being a tempo down also means that you can choose your setup one tempo later, thus remaining as flexible as possible.

2...g6!

Now I think Black is already slightly better. As I had noticed many times before, the relations between bishops g2/b7 and b2/g7 are always in favour of the kingside bishops. Wondering why it has always felt like that, I realized that it wasn't a mere feeling but an objective fact, as the kingside bishop is usually protected by the king after castling, which is an important detail.

3.♗b2 ♗g7 4.e4?!

And this is such a 'principled move'. As it turned out, however, taking this route isn't going to help White to complete his development in a harmonious way.

But I would also regard slow play as more than satisfactory, because I was looking forward to the idea of ...d6/...e5!?.

4.g4!? will hopefully be my next last-round game ☺.

4...d6

As my opponent had already spent nearly an hour, I decided not to disturb him any further and played this simple move pretty quickly.

I did burn a couple of minutes cursing myself for not having enough guts to play the wannabe brilliant ...e5!?, which was actually quite good as well. 4...e5!? (!!) – a free novelty for the readers. Since I knew I would be clearly better after the simple 4...d6, I eventually settled for the following line: 5.♘c3! (5.fxe5 ♘xe4! 6.♘f3 0-0 7.♕e2 ♘g5!; 5.♗xe5 0-0!, and after some thinking I realized that White is going to end up in an awkward position) 5...exf4 6.♕f3! 0-0 7.0-0-0

Anish Giri: 'As I had noticed many times before, the relations between bishops g2/b7 and b2/g7 are always in favour of the kingside bishops.'

with an unclear position, although I somehow prefer Black. But then again, I have bad associations with the ♕d1-f3 move, since Nigel Short managed to make this move in what seemed like a most inappropriate situation and as early as he could and yet crushed me in something like 20 moves. That was a couple of years back, but such memories stay with you and pop up whenever a sensible ♕d1-f3 appears in the position. Chess players never forget.

4...0-0! was even rougher. Now I missed that after 5.e5 ♘d5! 6.♕f3 I can win the necessary tempo with 6...♘b4! 7.♘a3 d6!, after which it's clear that Black is going to open up before White will manage h4, which worried me in case my ...d7-d6 would come too late.

5.♘f3

If 5.e5 then 5...♘d5!, which is an important move. Now I don't dis-

turb the harmony of my pieces, unlike in some lines of the Pirc, and have the added advantage of making the b2-bishop awkward. White is struggling to save himself here, having advanced too far without any strategy behind it.

5...0-0 6.♗d3 ♘c6

By now I had a one-hour lead on the clock and my position was clearly better. I did overestimate it a bit, but getting such a position out of the opening with black and being an hour up on the clock gave me a good excuse.

7.0-0 ♘b4

7...e5 was always my main idea, but when I saw that I could capture the bishop, I couldn't resist.

8.♕e2 b6!?

This is an interesting moment. Which useful move Black will play before

taking the bishop is mainly a matter of taste and style, I think. The player with the most sophisticated taste (his name starts with Hou and ends with dini) suggests the even more delicate 8...c6!?, preparing ...d5 or, in some lines, ...♕b6+ even.

9.a3

I considered 9.♘c3 the main move and intended to play 9...♗b7 10.♖ae1 a5!?, but just when I realized that White could play 11.f5 and take on d3 with the pawn, my opponent pleasantly surprised me with his move. Obviously, Black is better here too, as compared with some Grand Prix Attacks White's bishops are dead (one literally, one not), but maybe there is no need for ...a5.

9...♘xd3 10.♕xd3 ♗b7

Malmö 2012				1	2	3	4	5	6	7	8		cat. XVI
													TPR
1	**Fabiano Caruana**	IGM	ITA	2770	*	½	1	1	½	1	1	½	5½	2857
2	**Peter Leko**	IGM	HUN	2723	½	*	½	½	1	1	½	1	5	2792
3	**Anish Giri**	IGM	NED	2693	0	½	*	½	½	1	½	1	4	2688
4	**Nils Grandelius**	IGM	SWE	2556	0	½	½	*	½	½	1	1	4	2707
5	**Li Chao**	IGM	CHN	2703	½	0	½	½	*	0	1	½	3	2586
6	**Hans Tikkanen**	IGM	SWE	2566	0	0	0	½	1	*	0	1	2½	2554
7	**Jonny Hector**	IGM	SWE	2560	0	½	½	0	0	1	*	0	2	2499
8	**Emanuel Berg**	IGM	SWE	2587	½	0	0	0	½	0	1	*	2	2495

11.♗xf6

It's just funny that my passion for bishops made me so blind that I didn't even realize that this move was legal... 11.♘c3? ♘xe4!; 11.♖e1 is just awkward.

11...♗xf6 12.♘c3

Now I decided to start taking my time and punish my opponent for disrespecting his bishops.

12...♗g7

I like making such moves. You simply know that they are the best.

13.♖ae1

13...a5!?

I did realize that my position was merely slightly better, as even without bishops White has some space and a very solid position. I had the feeling the strongest move was 13...e5!? right away, but I really wanted to play the ...e5 break while keeping the queens on the board. Or at least try to.

After 13...e5 14.fxe5 (14.f5 gxf5 15. exf5 f6!) 14...dxe5 15.♕xd8 Black is slightly better, but White's position is hard to break and relatively easy to play (obviously up to some point).

14.♕e3?!

This one made me happy, but Emanuel was down to 20 minutes for the remaining 26 moves, so he was no longer paying attention to subtleties like that.

14.♖f2!? would probably make me go ...e5 anyway, as I was worried to run into f5 or e5 myself.

14...e5

It goes without saying that I wanted to open the diagonal for my b7-bishop with a slow plan like ...e6, ...♕d7, ...♖ae8, ...f5, but I was worried that my opponent would go e5 or f5 on the very next move.

15.f5!? I must say I had underestimated this move.

15.fxe5 dxe5 would give me what I wanted. I guess my next moves would be ...♕d7(6), ...♖ae8 and ...f5.

15...gxf5 16.exf5

Here I realized that even though I will be able to push ...d5, it will be met by d2-d4, which, even though Black is better, will make it a tough game for him if White manages to get something like ♘e2-g3 and c2-c3 in.

16...f6 The most solid move. I was worried that if I played just any move, I might get ♘e4!?, with the idea of meeting ...d5 with f6!.

16...d5 fails to the strong 17.f6! (17. ♘xe5? d4 18.♕g3 f6! made me very happy at first) 17...♗xf6 18.♘xe5 d4 19.♕g3+!.

17.d4 d5! I was slightly disappointed after 15.f5, but here I got happy again, as I saw the idea of ...c5, breaking through with my central pawns. However, after my opponent's last long think (after which he had no time left) I realized that if White played correctly, things would still be pretty tough.

18.dxe5?? A blunder, but the time-pressure was just getting too much. 18.♘e2! was the only way to keep things unclear.

Now my most tempting idea was surprisingly wrong: 18...c5?! 19.dxe5! d4 20.♕f4 fxe5, and now not the cooperative 21.♘xe5 ♕d5!, which I had calculated, but 21.♕g4!!, and White succeeds in getting the block on e4, nearly taking over:

ANALYSIS DIAGRAM

21...♔h8 (21...e4 22.♘g5!) 22.♘g3!. However, a more solid move like

18...♕d6!? would keep an edge for me: 19.a4 (19.♘g3 e4! 20.♘d2 ♕xa3 21.♘h5 ♖f7) 19...♔h8 (19...♖ae8 20. ♘g3; 19...c5!? 20.dxe5 fxe5 21.♘g5!) 20.♘g3 e4 21.♘d2 ♖g8, and while both bishops seem stupid for a second, after ...♗f8, ...c6, ...♗a6, ...♕d7, ...♗d6, etc., we will talk again. White, however, doesn't have any plan at all; c4, for example, will be calmly met by ...c6.

> 'I really enjoyed my piece coordination. Extra-piece coordination I should say.'

18...fxe5 19.f6

19.♘xe5 d4! 20.♕g3 dxc3, and fortunately the f6-square is over-protected.

19...♖xf6!

For some reason I had also missed this move, although when I eventually saw it, I realized that I was probably going to win a piece. After a few seconds of calculation I could leave out the word 'probably'.

20.♕xe5 ♖g6!

This calm move does the trick.
20...♖xf3?? 21.♕e6+!; 20...♖c6?? 21.♕xd5+.

21.♕f5?

21.♕f4! was the only way to create tricks, but after 21...♗xc3 22.♘h4!

ANALYSIS DIAGRAM

Black should still have an virtually winning advantage, especially after the accurate 22...♕d7! 23.♘xg6 hxg6 24.♕g3 ♕g7 25.♖e6 g5! 26.♖f5 ♗d4+ 27.♔h1 ♖f8! 28.♕f3 ♗c8! 29. ♖xf8+ ♔xf8 30.♕g6+ ♗g7, and Black should be winning.

21...♗xc3 22.♖e6 ♖g7!

23.h4 ♕f8 I really enjoyed my piece coordination. Extra-piece coordination I should say.
24.♕d3 ♕c5+ 25.♔h1 ♗a6 And here, without waiting for his flag and his rook to fall, Emanuel resigned. ∎

Novotnys and Queen Sacrifices

I
n studies with a lot of pieces on the board something can go wrong sometimes. In *The Art of the Endgame* I presented a correction of a study by Noam Manella from 1991. Next the Israeli composer sent me an enthusiastic email.

About his incorrect study Manella wrote: 'Gady Costeff tried to fix it, but afterwards it turned out to be incorrect again. So it seems that you closed a 20-year-old circle.'

That was indeed what it looked like. However, a little later I received a message from Aad Kortekaas, who informed me that there was something wrong with the initial position.

Manella, *The Problemist* 1991
(correction Timman 2011)
The Art of the Endgame page 78
White to play and win

What is the problem? Below I will give the solution in Kortekaas's own words.

I was forced to make a new version, which looks like this:

Manella, *The Problemist* 1991
(correction Timman 2012)
White to play and win

An additional advantage of the new version is that the variations are livelier.

1.e7 ♖e2 2.♘e4!!
The first Novotny[1]. Insufficient for the win was 2.♘xe2 because of 2...dxe2 3.♗xe2 h1♕ 4.♘b8 ♗b7 5.e8♕ ♘g6! 6.♕e3 ♕c1 7.♗d1 ♘b6 8.♕f3, and now White is in for a surprise:

ANALYSIS DIAGRAM

8...♕xb2+!! 9.♔xb2 ♘xc4+! 10.bxc4 ♗xf3, and the black king is out of danger.
2...♗xe4 3.e8♘!
Not 3.e8♕ in view of 3...♗b7! 4.♗xe2

h1♕ 5.♘e5 dxe5 6.♕xe5 ♕c1 7.♕c7 ♕h1, and White cannot win.
3...♗b7 4.♘c7! ♖e6

5.♘b8!! A real problem move.
5...d5 6.♘c6+!
The second Novotny. Black has two choices:
A) 6...♖xc6 7.♘xd5 mate
B) 6...♗xc6 7.♘xa6 mate
The promoted knight executes the mating moves.

The following study is another correction of a study from *The Art of the Endgame* (page 16)

Timman 2012
The Art of the Endgame
White to play and draw

The black king threatens to pick up the d-pawn, so that quick action is required.

1.f6! ♗xf6

1...♗f8 is followed by 2.♗d8 and 3.♗e7.

2.♗xd6 ♔c4

What to do now? If the d-pawn falls, the position looks theoretically lost.

3.♗g3!

The only good square for the bishop.

3...♔xd5 4.♗h4!!

The point of the previous move. The g-pawn is pinned. If Black captures the bishop, he will be left with the bishop of the wrong colour.

4...♗c3+!

A pretty counter-sacrifice that cannot be accepted either. The white king must be within the square of the g-pawn after the latter captures on h4.

5.♔d3!

The only square for the king. It has to keep attacking the enemy bishop.

5...h6

Protecting the g-pawn. Things look gloomy for White, but he has a resource.

6.f4!

Forcing the g-pawn to show its hand.

6...gxh4 7.♔e2 h3 8.♔f2!

The only good square for the king. After either 8.♔f1 ♗d4 or 8.♔f3 ♗e1!, it would be cut off.

8...♗e1+ 9.♔g1

Draw.

---

[1] Novotny: a piece is placed on the intersection between a diagonal of the opponent's bishop and a file (or rank) on which his rook operates

The chapter about mating patterns in *The Art of the Endgame* begins with a stunning idea of Alois Wotawa's.

But here's something even more stunning.

Timman 2011
(after Wotawa)
White to play and win

First the c-pawn has to be prevented from queening.

1.♖c6 b3

Now the b-pawn threatens to queen.

2.h6! Only with this intermediate pawn sacrifice can White win. After 2.♔d4 b2 3.♖g6 fxg6 4.♗e4+ ♔f4 5.♗xc2 gxh5 6.e3+ ♔g3 7.♗c3 h4 8.♗xb2 h3 9.♗e4 ♔f2! Black will manage to draw.

2...gxh6 3.♔d4! b2

4.♖g6!!

Wotawa's fantastic rook sacrifice.

4...fxg6 Forced, since 4...c1♕ 5.♗e4+ ♔f4 6.e3+ leads to a pure mate[2].

5.♗e4+ ♔f4 6.e3+!

The mating pattern has evaporated. Now White has to win a pawn race. But first he has to force the enemy king to a less favourable square.

6...♔g3 7.♗xc2 g5 8.e4

The race starts.

8...g4 9.e5 ♔h2 10.e6 g3 11.e7 g2 12.e8♕ Excelsior[3].

12...g1♕

13.♕e3! b1♕ 14.♗xb1 ♕xb1 15.♕xh6+ White concludes with a series of precise queen checks.

15...♔g2 16.♕g5+ ♔f1 17.♕f4+ ♔e1 18.♕e3+ And wins.

As an endgame study composer you always strive to improve existing ideas. In the next study I have refined the theme of mutual bishop promotion.

Timman 2012
White to play and win

Black has an extra rook, but he will be hard put to stop the white b-pawn.

1.f7!

Not 1.b6 at once because of 1...♖xc2 2.b7 ♖c4! 3.b8♕+ ♔g8 4.♕g3 and 4...♖e4 or 4...♗f7, and White cannot win. With the text-move White opens

---

[2] Pure mate: the squares available for the king are covered by only one enemy piece.

[3] Excelsior: the pawn, during the study, has travelled all the way from the second rank to its promotion square.

up the a1-h8 diagonal, ensuring that he will have a check on e5 later on.

1...♗xf7 2.b6 b3 The best chance.
3.♗d3!

The only good square for the bishop. The black rook has to be restricted in its movements as much as possible.

3...♖e2! This rook sacrifice frees the way for the passed b-pawn.

4.♗xe2 b2 5.♗d3 a2

6.♗b1! This blockading motif was demonstrated in a slightly different form by Stamma. **6...♗g8** Preparing a stalemate trap. **7.b7 a1♗!** The point of the previous move. **8.b8♗!!** A worthy reply to the bishop promotion. **8...♗c4 9.♗xa7 ♗d3** A final attempt. Now after 10.♗xd3?? b1♕ Black would win. **10.♗d4+** And wins.

Kotov and Mitrofanov composed a magnificent study in which a queen and rook chase each other while being en prise all the time. Their study intrigued me: could it be improved upon? To begin with, I succeeded in finding an attractive prelude.

Timman 2011
(extension of a study by Kotov and Mitrofanov)
White to play and draw

White's king is in danger. He has to sacrifice a rook.

1.♖f4+! ♔xf4 2.fxg7

After 2.♔g2 gxf6 Black is winning.

2...♔f3

Again the king is under threat. Now White has to sacrifice a bishop.

3.♗c6+!! White wants to open up the 7th rank for the rook.

3...dxc6 4.♖f7+ ♔e2 5.♖f8 ♔f1!

The situation around the white king is most threatening. Rigorous measures are called for.

6.g8♕ ♖xf8

7.c5! Introducing stalemate in the position. Black cannot take the promoted queen.

7...♖f7! The ritual in which the queen and rook keep clinging to each other commences.

8.♕g7!

The only way for White to cover squares g2 and h7.

8...♖f6!

Threatening a lethal check on h6, while at the same time preventing an enemy queen check.

9.♕g6!

Step by step the queen moves down the board.

9...♖f5!

And the rook follows suit.

10.♕g5! ♖f4! 11.♕g4!

Draw.

I thought the theme executed in this study so special, that I went searching for an even more impressive version with a new sacrifice of a promoted queen.

This search led to the following result.

Timman 2011
(dedicated to Yochanan Afek)
White to play and draw

Endgame study composers of renown are often honoured with a tourney when they celebrate a jubilee. However, for some reason there was no tourney on the occasion of Yochanan Afek's 60th birthday. That's why I have dedicated this study to him, as a present for his 60th birthday.

1.♖f1+ The only move, since after 1.e8♕ g2+ 2.♔g1 ♗h2+! 3.♔xh2 ♖h6+ White is mated.

1...♔e2 2.e8♕+ The first pawn that is promoted and then sacrificed.

2...♔xf1 3.♕g6! Kotov and Mitrofanov's scheme. **3...♖f5! 4.♕g5!**

Here it stalls. White threatens to take on f4, but he has no queen checks, which is why Black allows him to queen another pawn in order to break the stalemate.

4...♘c7 5.a8♕ d5! Not 5...♘xa8 6.a7, and Black faces the same problem again. With the text-move White cuts off the way for the new queen along the long diagonal. As White still has an a-pawn, stalemate motifs are not on the cards for the moment.

6.♕f8! Now a fascinating struggle

develops around square f4. Black still cannot take the queen on g5.

6...♘f6! Shielding off the f-file. 7.♕fxf6 now runs into 7...♖xf6 and Black wins. 7.g8♕ is insufficient, too, because of 7...♖xg5! 8.♕xg5 ♗xg5, and wins. However, White has an astonishing resource:

7.♕d6!! The third queen sacrifice. Square f4 remains the pivot of the position. Remarkably, the bishop stays motionless on this square, although it can capture two queens.

7...♘e6! The überdeckung theme gets a special dimension. Again White cannot queen a third pawn, since after 8.g8♕ Black wins with 8...♘xg5 9.♕xg5 and now 9...♘e4 or 9...♘g4, and the white queens are powerless against the devastating check on f2.

8.a7! Extremely cold-blooded. White leaves the clutter of pieces in the middle of the board alone and quietly advances his outside passed pawn. White wants to get a third queen, of course, but even more important is to vacate the a6-square for the queen on d6.

8...♖xg5 9.♕a6+ ♔f2 10.♕a2+ The black king has to be driven from its threatening position.

10...♔f3 11.♕g2+ ♔g4 12.♕e2+ This check is also necessary. After 12.a8♕ ♖h5+ 13.♔g1 ♗e3+ 14.♔f1 ♖f5+ 15.♔e1 ♗f2+ 16.♔d1 ♘xg7 Black is winning. In the long run the white queens stand no chance against the combined black forces.

12...♔h4 13.a8♕ Finally, White finds time to get a third queen.

13...♗e5

Finally a bishop move. Black vacates square f4 for the knight on e6. An im-

At the Modern Tretyakov Gallery world championship commentators Ilya Smirin and Jan Timman tried out the chess table of constructivist Alexander Rodchenko (original design 1925).

portant alternative was 13...g2+ – after 14.♕xg2 ♖xg2 15.♔xg2 ♘xg7 16.♕f8! ♘ge8 17.♕xb4 White will just be able to maintain the balance.

14.g8♕! White has to get a fourth queen. The alternative 14.♕f8 was insufficient because of 14...♘f4 15.♕e1 ♗c3 16.♕d6 ♘h5, and Black can reinforce his position with decisive effect. Strictly speaking, with this fourth queen promotion the study has come to an end. Black has to take the queen, leaving White with two waterproof roads to a draw. As this is a present, I have tried to use the most attractive way to end this study.

14...♘xg8 15.♕c8 The alternative 15.♕xd5 would do as well.

15...♘f4 16.♕h2+! gxh2 17.♕h3+!

The final queen sacrifice. No matter how Black captures, it's stalemate.
The lone white king is left surrounded by an enormous army of black pieces.

Remarkably enough, White has not captured a single enemy piece in the course of the entire study.

Now let's return to the first diagrammed position, my first attempt to correct Manella's study.

The position is illegal; in other words, it could not have come about in a legal manner. The proof of its illegality runs as follows:
1. Black has eight pawns and, besides his king, four pieces. So only three pieces have been captured.
2. White has seven pawns and, besides his king, four pieces. So only a maximum of four pieces and a (promoted) pawn can have been captured.
3. The white pawns have captured three black pieces (b3, c4 and h5, one capture each), so this is possible.
4. However, the black pawns have made a minimum of five captures of a piece or a pawn, to wit a5 or a6 once, the d-pawns together four times. This is possible, but in that case the black pawn on h2 should have reached that square without capturing anything. However, in order to 'pass' the white h-pawn, this pawn must have been captured by a black piece. Which leaves only four white pieces to be captured by pawns, which is one too few.
   Particularly the final part of the reasoning is difficult to follow, but it does make sense. ∎

Tales from Thailand

I first visited Thailand back in 2004, at a time when the country barely registered on the chess radar. The trip came about when I asked the then British Ambassador to Greece, David Madden – who by fortuitous circumstance happened to play on my cricket team – whether he had any contacts in the country, as I fancied popping in, as one does, on my way back from China. He did, as it turned out, and a pretty good one – the British Club, in Bangkok, which by coincidence happened to be celebrating its centenary. This venerable institution – an oasis of calm among the hurly-burly of the teeming capital, on a large, central plot of land, gifted by the King of Siam – held all manner of traditional English sporting activities but, alas, not chess. Thankfully the President of the Club, David Quine, was very receptive to the innovative idea of a simul and quickly found over a dozen members who relished the idea of facing a GM. The rest of the places were filled up by inviting players from the established Bangkok Chess Club (BCC), which, at the time, was more or less the only club in Thailand. The evening went superbly well, with a beautiful, large ice-sculpture of a chess piece unveiled at the start (a brave idea, considering the humid cli-

mate). Unlike my esteemed colleague Garry Kasparov, I don't restrict the strength of opposition to Elo <2000, as fly-swatting makes poor spectator sport. I won most of the games, as usual, but local honour was proudly upheld when I dropped the odd half and even full point here and there.

My second visit, this time to the Thai Stock Exchange for two simuls, arose from the contact I had made with Kai Tuorila, an expatriate Finn and dynamo of the BCC. As on the previous occasion, the trip was conceived as an add-on to another Far Eastern sojourn. The event was successful, providing not only pleasure for the fans, but also attracting some TV coverage. The sponsorship from the world of finance seemed particularly promising but, alas, as is so often the case, it was unfortunately not to be repeated.

In my unlikely capacity as the national coach of the Islamic Republic of Iran, I paid another visit to Bangkok in 2007, a stop-over en route, from Tehran, to the Asian Indoor Games in Macau. Quite why one would arrange the journey in such a cumbersome manner – other than to provide the officials with an opportunity for a damned good night out – I really don't know. In Doha, the previous year, the top Iranian officials were ensconced – not entirely coincidentally, one suspects – in one of the handful of hotels in the city that served alcohol. By chance, I also stayed in this fine establishment (I should really have been at the Athletes' Village with all the

other coaches, but that is another lengthy story...). When engaged for an important job, I take my responsibilities very seriously, but even I could not help notice that the hotel bar was frequented by a disproportionately large number of young, single Philippinas. Call me deeply cynical, if you wish, for suspecting the guardians of Islamic values of hypocrisy, but let's say I was not in the least surprised when it was suddenly announced, as we prepared to depart Bangkok, we were to be 'unexpectedly' detained a further 24 hours, due to the unavailability of flights...

My four most recent visits have all been in conjunction with the Thailand Open – now in its 12th edition – which alternates each year between Bangkok and other resorts. In 2002, 2003, 2009 and 2011 the tournament was held in Pattaya, which developed rapidly from a sleepy village to provide rest and recreation for American troops during the Vietnam War, and which now surely has a strong claim to be the sleaziest place on the planet. The area around Walking Street, in particular, offers a super-abundance of debauchery, sufficient to attract not a few anonymous GMs, regardless of whether or not a tournament is taking place. By comparison, the red-light district of Amsterdam is rather like a convent.

Of course, Thailand offers far more than base pleasures of the loins – palaces, temples, food and shopping are just a few of the numerous attractions – and this is partly why the flagship tournament has grown steadily in both fame and numbers from very humble beginnings. The real reason, however, is the great team of hardworking organisers, led by Kai Tuorila, who do a fantastic job with very limited financial resources. Yes, let it be stressed, this is no Gibraltar Open. Sponsorship is increasing, but in a country where 'makruk', or Thai chess, remains more popular, it is an uphill task. What the Thailand Open does offer, though, is a very warm welcome and a wonderful experience for the amateur player. The venues are invariably luxury hotels which, as anyone who has travelled in South East Asia knows, are generally far superior to their European equivalents. My only real complaint, apart from the rather modest prize-fund, is the double rounds. No GM wishes to squander his hard-earned Elo points through fatigue, but it is also hard to understand why any tourist, eager for sightseeing or simply relaxing on holiday, would wish to be chained to the board all day either. Every year I preach the same sermon on the evils of double rounds to Kai. He listens politely, but then explains why it cannot be any different. He is completely wrong, of course, and eventually my good friend will realise it ☺.

In 2012 we were back in Bangkok, at the prestigious Dusit Thani Hotel, home to royalty and countless celebrities over the decades. Jan Gustafsson returned in a bid to defend his title, but the star attraction, this time, was women's world champion Hou Yifan. The Chinese teenager gave a simul at Government House prior to the event and met with Prime Minister Yingluck Shinawatra – a breakthrough in recognition for what, as I have mentioned, is very much a minority sport. Her diplomatic triumph, however, was not quite matched by exploits on the board. Hou's uneven play, on the back of a disappointing Chinese Champi-

onship, indicated that her phenomenal result in Gibraltar has not yet brought a permanent shift to a higher plateau. She survived big scares against FM Martin Voigt and the veteran Finnish GM Yrjo Rantanen, beating the former and drawing with the latter, and dropped a further half point to the modestly rated Philippino Sander Severino (as did I, in fact). Her dreams of victory, however, only suffered a fatal blow in the seventh round:

Short-Hou Yifan
Bangkok 2012
position after 20...♘c5

The opening – a Queen's Indian – had not gone particularly well for me. My congealed mass of central pawns was vulnerable and unable to advance. I did not fancy the prospect of allowing the very dangerous exchange sacrifice 21.♗g4 ♕xe4!. Lacking any decent alternatives, I therefore jettisoned a pawn.

21.♗xc5 ♗xc5 22.♗g4 ♗xe3+ 23.♔h1 f5?!

Inexperience. One has to know when to defend actively and when to defend passively. This is a time for passive defence. There was no harm in play-

ing 23...♖cd8 24.♗e6+ ♔h8 25.♖f3 ♗c5 26.♖h3 g6, as checkmate is not at all imminent. Certainly Black will have to endure some pressure and abandon the plan of queening a pawn for a while, but it is not clear how White can achieve anything. Long-term Black is sitting pretty.

24.♗xf5

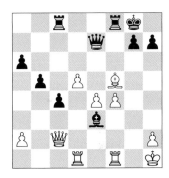

24...♖cd8?

But this is too much. Yifan obviously intended to sacrifice the exchange, but then changed her mind. During the game I thought it was total crap, but actually 24...♖xf5 25.exf5 c3! is still not so clear.

25.e5 ♔h8 26.♕e4 ♕c5 27.♗xh7

Black's game is in total ruins. My technique for the remaining moves was very far from optimal but, with such an overwhelming advantage, it was beyond even my talent to let slip the win.

27...c3 28.♗g6 c2 29.♕g2 ♗xf4 30.♗xc2 ♕e7 31.d6 ♕e6 32. ♖de1 g5 33.♖f3 g4 34.♖f2 ♕h6 35.♕xg4 ♗xe5 36.♖xe5 ♖xf2 37.♖h5 ♖xd6 38.♖xh6+ ♖xh6 39.♕c8+ ♔g7 40.♕c7+ ♖f7 41.♕g3+ ♔f8 42.h4 ♖hf6 43.♗b3 ♖f1+ 44.♔g2 ♖7f6 45.h5 1-0

The early front-runner, perhaps a little surprisingly, was the Indian IM M.R.Venkatesh, who started with an impressive five straight wins. However, after he succumbed to your columnist on the white side of an English Opening in Round 6, the lead changed hands irrevocably. I effectively sealed victory with a slice of good fortune in the penultimate round:

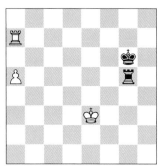

Short-Amonatov
position after 68.♖xa7

I had squandered a substantial if not to say decisive advantage in the middlegame, and through some further imprecise endgame play rather ineptly stumbled my way here. Many readers will recognize the key elements of the Vancura position, whereby Black draws by attacking the a-pawn from the side and checking the king away from supporting the a-pawn. By coincidence, imme-

diately prior to this tournament I had been coaching in Kuala Lumpur and, on the very first day, had shown my pupils this essential defensive method. Little did I imagine that the basic position would appear so soon...

68...♔f6?!

This doesn't actually lose, but it is a big step in the wrong direction (believe it or not, in a number of lines Black needs to control the h-file!) and shows that my opponent – Tajikistan's finest player and rated over 2600 – did not have the vital knowledge at his fingertips. Instead something like 68...♖b5 would do fine, followed by switching the rook to the f-file as the white king approaches. If 69.a6 Black plays 69...♖b6!. Incidentally, Anatoly Karpov gave me a rather annoying practical demonstration of this idea in Game 3 of our 1992 Candidates' match – a game I botched up completely.

69.a6

69...♖a5?

Now it was already difficult. The only move to hold was 69...♖d5! – which is not at all easy when you have been under pressure for hours, you desperately need a cigarette and you are down to 30 seconds a move.

70.♖a8!

The only winning move, preventing the black king from approaching the pawn.

70...♖a4 71.♔d3 ♔g7 72.♔c3

By a most improbable coincidence, I had also shown my Malaysian pupils a nearly identical position from the rightly-lauded *Nunn's Chess Endings Volume II*. The only difference was that the white king was worse placed on c2, with the black rook on a3. There Black to move can only draw by ...♖h3!! – which is almost impossible to find, unless you know it. Here, though, Black is busted.

72...♖f4

Trying to head back to the Vancura position, which I suspect all along had been in Amonatov's mind – albeit a touch hazily. It is all too late now. Smug in the knowledge of how to win, I was able to instantly bash out

73.♖a7+! ♔g6 74.♖b7 ♖a4 75. a7 ♔f6 76.♔b3 ♖a1 77.♔c4 ♔e6 78.♔c5 1-0

The white king meanders down to b8. Perhaps there is something to be said for endgame study after all? ■

Forcing Moves

1

Mendoza-Sanchez
Khanty-Mansiysk 2010

Black threads the needle with the exciting coup de grace **1...♖xf5! 2.♕xf5** 2.exf5 ♖e8+ 3.♔d2 ♕xb2+ 4.♔d3 ♕e2+. **2...♕xb2 0-1**

2

Sorokina-Shlakich
Russia 2008

A fascinating special case is the 're-constituted' ♕+♖ ending resulting from mutual promotion. Formerly rare (because they scare our socks off) these hyper-tactical solutions are seen more often now (computers don't wear socks!). **1...a1♕ 2.♖g8+!** This clever ruse narrows Black's margin of error. **2...♔h6** 2...♔xg8?? 3.d8♕+ and 4.♕xg5+, perpetual. **3.d8♕ ♕d4+!** Amazingly the only winning move. **4.♔f3** Best try. 4.♔g2 ♕e4+ 5.♔h3 ♕f5+ is trivial. Now **4...♕d3+ 5.♔g4 f5+ 6.♔h3 ♕f1# 0-1**, but the game went like GM Wilder's old 'Agony' column: 4...♖f1+ 5.♔g4?? (5.♔g2!) 5...♕d1+?? (clearly Black intended 5...♖xf4+! 6.gxf4? ♕xf4+ 7.♔h3 ♕f3# but only now saw 6.♔h3! – by pure

chance 6...♖f5! saves all: 7.♕e7 ♕d3. Now Wilder might conclude, 'Black feels like a horse's buttocks') 6.♔f5 ♕d3+ 7.♔f6 ♕d4+ 8.♔xf7 1-0.

3

Nimzowitsch-Capablanca
New York 1927

Vultures circle when ♕+♖ invade the back row. The defender must anticipate so many threats, zugzwang becomes a problem: **1...♖c1!** Or 1...♖b1/a1. **2.♖e3** King moves allow 2...♖c2!; 2.♕e2 ♕g1+ or 2.h3 ♖g1+ 3.♔h4 ♖g4 mate. Most stubborn was 2.♖d3 ♖f1 3.♕d2, but Rybka eats White for lunch: 3...h4+! 4.♔xh4 ♖d1! 5.♕e2 (5.♕xd1 ♕xh2+ 6.♖h3 ♕xf4+) 5...♖xd3 6.♕xd3 ♕xh2+ and mate. **2...♖f1 0-1** 3.♕g2 ♖g1, or 3.♕-other ♕g1+.

4

Karpov-Taimanov
Moscow 1972

1.♕c1! was a clock-stopper: **1...♕a2 2.♘g5+ ♔h8 3.♕xf7+ ♔h7 4.♕g5 ♕b1+ 5.♔h2 1-0.** 6.♕g6+! and mate (or 5...g6 6.♕h6 mate).

5

Gufeld-Kortchnoi
Moscow 1961

Key squares hang in the balance, and Kortchnoi finds the forcing/positional retreat **1...♕f8!** locking in White's liabilities, including the tell-tale exposed monarch: **2.♖de1** If 2.♕xa7, both 2...♖xf3 and 2...♕f5 win. **2...♕f5 3.♔h2 d4!** Already a pawn falls and White is busted. Justice is swift in the 'fourth phase'! **4.♕e2 ♖h4 5.♕g2 ♖g6 0-1**

6

Balinas-Kortchnoi
Lugano 1968

1...♗xc3! begs to be played. **2. bxc3 ♖h6 3.f3** Or 3.f4 ♖xg3+ 4.♔h1 ♖xe3. **3...♖xg3+ 4.♔h1** Did the Filipino GM hallucinate mate or lack the stomach for Victor's grindstone? Better was 4.hxg3 ♕h1+ 5.♔f2 ♖h2+ 6.♔g2 ♖xg2+ 7.♔e3 ♖xe2+ 8.♔xe2, and the win is still far from trivial. **4...exf3!** Now White goes down in flames. **5.♕b2 ♖g2 6.♕b8+ ♔g7 7.♘f5+ ♕xf5 8. ♖g1 ♕h3 9.♕e5+ ♔f7 10.♕f4+ ♔g6 0-1**

Ray Robson

CURRENT ELO: 2614

DATE OF BIRTH: 25 October 1994

PLACE OF BIRTH: Tumon, Guam

PLACE OF RESIDENCE: Clearwater, Florida, USA

What is your favourite colour?
I don't really have one now, but it used to be green.

What food makes you happy?
My mom's food.

And what drink?
In general I like juices, but I have no specific preferences.

Who is your favourite author?
Mark Twain or Ray Bradbury.

What was the most interesting book you ever read?
Chess Child ☺ (The Story of Ray Robson by Dr Gary Robson, Ray's father – ed.)

What is your all-time favourite movie?
Compared to most people, I don't think I've seen a lot of movies. *Hot Fuzz* was fun, though.

What is your favourite TV series?
The Twilight Zone was quite interesting.

Do you have a favourite actor?
No, I need to develop one.

And a favourite actress?
Ditto.

What music do you like to listen to?
Classic hits from the 60s and 70s. I even like some pop music. The only type of music I don't really listen to is rap.

Do you have a favourite painter?
No, but only because I have never been very interested in art for some reason.

What was the best game you ever played?
My game against Rasmussen from the Arctic Chess Challenge in 2009 is one of the most memorable.

Who is your favourite chess player of all time?
Garry Kasparov. He played dynamic and correct chess at the same time.

Is there a chess book that had a profound influence on you?
There was not one book that really influenced my style, but I learned a lot of chess history from Garry Kasparov's *My Great Predecessors* series.

What was the most exciting chess game you ever saw?
Gashimov-Grischuk and Mamedyarov-Sutovsky from the World Team Championships 2010 were both exciting to watch.

What is the best chess country?
From the places I've been to, Russia or the Netherlands.

What are chess players particularly good at?
Chess players are supposed to be good at poker, but I'm not one of them.

Do chess players have typical shortcomings?
Some chess players can be socially awkward, or tend to overanalyse things. They can also be too self-centred.

Do you have any superstitions concerning chess?
Not really. I sometimes have small superstitions, but I try to get rid of them.

I do often use the same pen if I am winning, though.

Who or what would you like to be if you weren't yourself?
I would like to be some kind of cat, perhaps a tiger or a liger.

Which three people would you like to invite for dinner?
There are too many possibilities! Stephen Hawking, Roger Federer, and Jim Carrey would be an interesting mix.

Is there something you'd love to learn?
I'd love to learn more languages, and also to be less uptight at times.

What is your greatest fear?
That something will happen to the people closest to me.

What would you save from your house if it were on fire?
My wallet, my passport, and my computer.

If you could change one thing in the chess world, what would it be?
It would be great if chess was more popular.

What is the stupidest rule in chess?
En passant, followed by castling.

What will be the nationality of the 2050 chess world champion?
No idea. Cyborg?

Is a knowledge of chess useful in everyday life?
Not too much.